RECLAIMING A MISSION

RECLAIMING A MISSION

New Direction for the Church-Related College

by

Arthur J. De Jong

William B. Eerdmans Publishing Company
Grand Rapids, Michigan

Copyright © 1990 by Wm. B. Eerdmans Publishing Co.
255 Jefferson Ave. S.E., Grand Rapids, Mich. 49503

Printed in the United States of America

Library of Congress Cataloging-in-Publication Data

De Jong, Arthur J.
    Reclaiming a mission: new direction for the church-related
college / by Arthur J. De Jong.
       p.   cm.
   ISBN 0-8028-0436-5
    1. Church colleges—United States—History. 2. Church and
college—United States.   3. Universities and colleges—United
States. I. Title.
LC621.D4   1990
378.73—dc20   90-32554
                                         CIP

This book is dedicated to my parents,
Peter (deceased) and Anna De Jong

Contents

CONTENTS

III APPLICATION OF NEW PRINCIPLES

Introduction

This book is directed to the mainline Protestant denominations and their affiliated colleges. I have borrowed Martin Marty's categories:

- Colonial: Congregational, Presbyterian, and Episcopal
- Frontier: Methodist, Disciples of Christ, and Northern Baptist
- Continental: Lutheran and Reformed.[1]

Taken together, these denominations and their affiliated colleges are called mainline Protestant. Many of the points made in the book may apply to other denominations and their colleges, including fundamentalist denominations and their colleges, as well as the Roman Catholic Church and its colleges. Material in the book may also be helpful to seminaries. However, the book is directed mostly to these mainline Protestant denominations and their colleges because these are the denominations and colleges with which I am most familiar. I shall be pleased if this book proves helpful to other denominations and their colleges.

1. Martin E. Marty, "Transpositions: American Religion in the 1980s," Wade Clark Roof, ed. for *Religion in American Society,* special issue of *The Annals of the American Academy of Political and Social Science,* Richard D. Lambert and Alan W. Heston, eds. 480 (July 1985): 13.

INTRODUCTION

In contrast to the pre–World War II years when the private, liberal arts, church-related college provided the model for higher education, after World War II the church-related liberal arts colleges lost their leadership role to the rapidly growing urban public universities. In surrendering their leadership role to the large public universities, the church-related colleges lost their uniqueness, their *raison d'être,* and they began to model themselves after the large universities. To begin with, the secular winds blowing in these universities began to blow in the church-related colleges as well. Second, the structure of the universities, based upon a distinct separation of the academic disciplines and specialization in those disciplines, was adopted by the church-related colleges. Instead of attempting to influence the total lives of their students as they had in the past, the church-related colleges adopted from the secular universities the concept of a "value-free" approach to the educational process; as a result, the impact of the church-related colleges on the moral and spiritual dimension of students was greatly diminished. During these years many of the colleges and their denominations parted company, or at least grew far apart.

The purpose of this book is to ask these denominations and their affiliated colleges to rethink this position to which they have come, to urge these colleges to develop once again a distinct and meaningful *raison d'être.*

At the close of the twentieth century the context in which these denominations and their colleges are functioning is very different from that of earlier decades and centuries. In the past, these mainline Protestant denominations shaped American society, including the American government. In exchange, American society, including the American government, developed many subtle ways of supporting these mainline Protestant denominations. That mutually supportive relationship no longer exists. In addition, if America was once a religious nation, its religious point of view has given way to a secular point of view. Furthermore, if America was once primarily Christian in its religious preference, it is fast losing this flavor and is rapidly becoming pluralistic. The context in which the mainline Protestant denominations and their colleges are living has changed, but these denominations and their colleges have not fully realized these changes. Thus their response to contemporary society is no longer appropriate. If there is to be a new *raison d'être* for these church-related colleges, it will be achieved only when they have grasped more fully our changed context, when they realize more fully how captive they have become to the model provided by the large, secular universities, and when they ground themselves upon Christian tenets and a paradigm consistent with those tenets. The changed context compels the church-related colleges to regain their integrity, unique identity, and mission. The church must present its point of view in the marketplace of ideas called higher education. In partnership, these denominations and their colleges must be a presence in contemporary higher education.

The book is divided into three parts. Part I describes what happened after World War II in American society, in the mainline Protestant denominations, and in higher education. It concludes with a critical analysis of the public university, the church-related college, and the relationship between the mainline Protestant denominations and American higher education. Part II prescribes a new *raison d'être* for the church-related college by pointing it to basic Christian tenets and toward the post-modern science paradigm, and by asking the church-related colleges to develop a new relationship with our pluralistic society.

Some language in the book may need definition and clarification. The phrase "liberal arts" is a shortened version of the phrase "liberal arts and sciences." Some people mistake the shorter term to refer to a curriculum which is comprised only of the humanities and arts. When I use the phrase "liberal arts," I mean a full curriculum of the natural sciences, social sciences, the humanities, and the fine arts.

Throughout the book I have chosen to use the word "Cartesian-Newtonian" to describe a paradigm which formed as the result of the work of Descartes and Newton. Others may use the phrase "classical science" to cover the same period. And I have chosen to use the phrase "post-modern science" to refer to those scientific theories and that paradigm which began to form in the late nineteenth century and which continue to gather strength at the present time. These are merely the labels I have chosen; they do not represent any departure from accepted theory.

Finally, throughout the book I have used the phrase "church-related" in referring to the colleges affiliated with the mainline Protestant denominations. This is simply because this phrase historically was used by these denominations for their colleges and by these colleges to refer to themselves.

While I take full responsibility for the contents of the book, I want to express my gratitude to some special people and groups. I am grateful to the Board of Trustees of Muskingum College who gave me a three-month leave to rest from nine years of the presidency at Muskingum. To Dr. James I. McCord, Chancellor of the Center of Theological Inquiry in Princeton, New Jersey, I wish to say thanks for providing me with a quiet place to read, think, and write. Thanks also to my colleagues at the Center for their interest and support, especially to Dr. Russell Stannard, a visiting fellow from England. Dr. David Watermulder and Ruth Watermulder from Bryn Mawr, Pennsylvania, gave me encouragement to pursue the book, along with their friendship, as did Dr. Thomas Gillespie of Princeton Seminary. I am grateful to Joyce De Jong and Deborah Leinan, who helped to put the manuscript into publishable form.

Whitworth College   ARTHUR J. DE JONG
Summer 1989

I. A Diagnosis of Our Present Situation

1. American Society after World War II

Four major themes will be addressed in this chapter. First, I will describe the growth in size and influence of the American higher education enterprise. Second, I will show how European pessimism gained a foothold in America and how this pessimism has been strengthened by self-doubt and cynicism created by the Vietnam War, Watergate, economic recessions, and the intense competition which America faces in the world economic community. Third, I will describe the changed value system and basis of morality which has come to dominate American society. Finally, I will discuss the overall impact which these changes seem to be having on Americans, particularly American youth.

THE GROWTH IN SIZE AND IMPORTANCE OF HIGHER EDUCATION

One of the most significant developments in America after World War II has been the rapid growth in size and importance of the institutions of higher education. America has always favored higher education. The early founding of the colonial colleges shows that Americans held education in high esteem right from the start. As Americans pushed back the frontier, they just as quickly founded colleges. The number and variety of colleges now dotting the American landscape is evidence of the high esteem in which we hold education. Yet prior to World War II,

3

higher education was considered appropriate for only a relatively small percentage of America's youth.

Some distinct changes related to higher education took place in American society after World War II. I'll only mention them briefly now; they will be discussed in greater depth in chapter 3. First, the GIs changed the notion of who went to college. With the GIs' return from war, a college education was no longer reserved for the elite of American youth, but opened up to any American youth who wished to attend. The principle of "equal access," propelled by federal financial aid, soon became a reality. Second, the size of the generation following the GIs—the "baby boom" generation—led to a population explosion in higher education. Third, higher education was tied to the notion of opportunity and upward mobility. These three changes caused higher education to reach an all-time high in numbers, importance, and esteem in the minds and value systems of Americans. A messianic flavor infused Americans' view of higher education. The fact that colleges and universities doubled, tripled, even quadrupled in size seemed to cement in place this new position of higher education in American society.

In the 1970s and 1980s, America's attitude toward higher education changed from a love affair to a love-hate relationship. The violence of the late sixties and early seventies and the downturn of America's economy brought a periodic change in attitude toward higher education. Yet the demographers' predictions that colleges and universities would shrink in size because of fewer high-school students available for college did not come to pass. "Nontraditional" students began flocking into institutions of higher education at record numbers, not only helping colleges and universities to keep their enrollment levels from falling, but significantly changing the average age of the college student. It appears that, in spite of the current criticism of higher education, this influx of nontraditional students will at least sustain, if not increase, the level of population in America's colleges and universities until the end of this century. Finally, the new economic competition in which America is now engaged with other countries appears to be enough to maintain, if not increase, the interest in higher education that we have seen develop in the decades since World War II.

THE GROWTH OF PESSIMISM AND SELF-DOUBT

In the seventies, America began to be infected with widespread self-doubt and pessimism. The height of optimism in America was reached during the Kennedy administration a decade earlier, when America seemed to believe it was living in the mythical city of Camelot. Arthur Levine describes the major features of that era: "the sense of voluntarism, the perception of mutuality of individual and community interest, and the belief in the individual's ability to profit from cooperation with the community."[1] Ringing in the ears of all Americans, but especially America's youth, were the words of President John F. Kennedy: "Ask not what your country can do for you; ask what you can do for your country." America's optimism was at its peak and it was a corporate optimism; it was a belief that persons banding together in community could alter the course of society, indeed of the world. It was an attractive ideal, which gave birth to the Peace Corps. Even though the world had its share of ailments— the Cuban missile crisis was a scary moment in history— nevertheless there was a belief that the world could be made into a better, safer place. A significant share of this optimism was based upon the belief that education would make rational citizens who, through corporate good will, would act to reform the world. It was from this peak that America began a long slide into pessimism, self-doubt, and the disintegration of community and corporate responsibility.

Pessimism had already been endemic in Europe for some time. Friedrich Nietzsche had pronounced in Europe a century earlier, with his dictum "God is dead," that the Christian understanding of God is no longer tenable. Freud contributed to the

---

1. Arthur Levine, *When Dreams and Heroes Died: A Portrait of Today's College Student* (San Francisco: Jossey-Bass, 1980), p. 10.

undermining of the traditional Christian underpinnings of the Western world in the early twentieth century by explaining human emotions and activity in a totally new way that left God out. Marcel Proust and James Joyce claimed that man does not have personal responsibility for his actions. Karl Marx pointed to a new authority, again without the traditional transcendent authority, by claiming that economics is the basis of human society. Artists joined philosophers, poets, economists, and psychiatrists in assuming the passing of the old order by experimenting with new forms of expression, including cubism, expressionism, surrealism, and futurism.

In America, Einstein established his theory of relativity, undercutting the earlier common understanding of our world. Paul Johnson describes the massive implications of Einstein: "He lived to see moral relativism, to him a disease, become a social pandemic, just as he lived to see his fatal equation bring into existence nuclear warfare. . . . The public response to relativity was one of the principal formative influences on the course of twentieth-century history. It formed a knife, inadvertently wielded by its author, to help cut society adrift from its traditional moorings in the faith and morals of Judeo-Christian culture."[2] Paul Johnson sums up the impact of relativity when he says that it was "the end of the old order, with an unguided world adrift in a relativistic universe."[3]

In the 1970s this pessimism hit America, particularly American youth. Coming on the heels of the optimistic sixties, it was a massive jolt to the American mind and spirit. The institutions which might have moderated this contrasting spirit—the family and the schools—were themselves under attack and in decline. This made the American experience of pessimism all the more acute.

College students of the seventies were very different from their counterparts in the sixties. Levine quotes one such student

2. Paul Johnson, *Modern Times: The World from the Twenties to the Eighties* (New York: Harper & Row, 1983), pp. 4-5.
3. *Ibid.*, p. 48.

6

as saying: "We're not real college kids like the people who went to school in the 1960s."[4] Far from feeling that they could change the world, college students in the seventies felt that their world was falling apart. There was a deep distrust of all social institutions, from large corporations to the church, and a sense that these social institutions were somewhat immoral or dishonest. Instead of facing outward as the students of the sixties had, the students of the seventies turned inward as their way of handling a hostile, untrustworthy, and immoral world. As Levine states: "For many the one remaining refuge is 'me.'"[5] In just one decade America's youth went from an outwardly directed optimism to narcissism. Again quoting Levine: "Like Aristotle's old men, today's college students live in a time when dreams and heroes have died."[6]

Contributing to America's pessimism is "the bomb" and the subsequent arms race. Robert L. Heilbroner describes our dilemma well: "There is a question in the air, more sensed than seen, like the invisible approach of a distant storm, a question that I would hesitate to ask aloud did I not believe it existed unvoiced in the minds of many: 'Is there hope for man?' In another era such a question might have raised thoughts of man's ultimate salvation or damnation. But today the brooding doubts that it arouses have to do with life on earth, now, and in the relatively few generations that constitute the limit of our capacity to imagine the future."[7] Ingrid Canright, referring to the reaction of Americans to our nuclear world, asks: "Why is it too much? The world's been in bad shape before," and then offers the following answer: "We face a world in which a threat greater than any war hangs over us every day, a threat so terrifying that it inspires political positions as irrational as they are divergent. We are not united on the nuclear issue. Worse, most of us are paralyzed by it. You can look at the possibility of nuclear war as one hell of a

4. Levine, p. 1.
5. *Ibid.*, p. 21.
6. *Ibid.*, p. 26.
7. Robert L. Heilbroner, *An Inquiry into the Human Prospect* (New York: W. W. Norton and Company, 1974), p. 13.

reason to become politically active. Or you can look at it as one hell of an excuse for apathy."[8] Listen again to Robert Heilbroner: "If any single happening of our age has made its impact felt upon this nation, it is the prospect of mass destruction to which we are now exposed. . . . With brutal abruptness the new war technology has knocked out the keystone of our optimistic philosophy by forcing us to confront the possibility of national extinction, an eventuality which has never before even remotely entered our calculations."[9]

While the threat of nuclear war provides the most pervasive reason for pessimism, recent national events have also contributed to pessimism and cynicism in contemporary American society. In fact, a series of national events—namely, the Vietnam War, Watergate, and, more recently, the Iran-Contra scandal—have cast a pall over America.

To the students of the seventies, Vietnam was not simply an unpopular war; it was an immoral war. Martin Luther King, Jr., risked his already precarious stature in America by viewing his crusade for civil rights and his opposition to the Vietnam War as one and the same issue. He joined them around his view of "the fundamental meaning of America." Of the Vietnam War he wrote, "No one who has any concern for the integrity and life of America today can ignore the present war. If America's soul becomes totally poisoned, part of the autopsy must read Vietnam."[10] King was among the first to predict that this war would exact a heavy toll, not only in deaths and casualties among those fighting there, but in the soul of America. He made that prediction in 1967. Unfortunately, the prediction of cynicism resulting from the Vietnam War has been all too accurate. William H. Becker captures the dilemma faced by those soldiers who disagreed with the war in which they were fighting: "For many combat veterans, fighting a

8. Ingrid Canright, "What Has Nuclear War Got to Do with Romance?" *The Chronicle of Higher Education,* 5 June 1985, p. 72.

9. Robert L. Heilbroner, *The Future as History* (New York: Harper & Bros., 1960), pp. 61-62.

10. Martin Luther King, Jr., "Beyond Vietnam: Or Martin Luther King's Prophecy for the '80's," *Clergy and Laity Concerned* (1982): 2-3.

brutal but meaningless war eroded their confidence in the values for which they had understood themselves to be fighting. If America sent them to fight *this* war, then perhaps America was different from what they had thought. Usually it was only after returning to the States, sometimes many years afterward, that the veteran realized how much his trust in his country had been eroded or destroyed."[11] William Ehrhart came back from Vietnam totally confused, saying to his mother: "Everything's, well, just different. I don't know what happened, Mom. It feels like I finally managed to escape from Jupiter—and I've ended up on Mars. 'Ehrhart to Earth, Ehrhart to Earth'—and nobody answers. I've ended up on Mars."[12]

For many people the Vietnam War symbolizes the moment when America gave up being the champion of idealism and morality in the world and was lured into pursuing power instead. Unfortunately, it was not just Americans becoming disappointed in their country; there was worldwide disappointment in America. Normally it is the youth of a nation who have the lion's share of the nation's idealism. Certainly that was true in the sixties. Thus it was all the more stark a contrast to the sixties when American youth lost their idealism during the seventies.

The nation had just begun to handle some of the emotions resulting from the Vietnam War when the event called Watergate took place. The nation saw a president and his aides so blinded by the desire for power that they set aside common ethical behavior in search of self-aggrandizement. As Arthur Levine concludes: "The most serious consequence of the Vietnam/Watergate era is not the cynicism, the decreasing interest in politics, or even the turning inward of young people but rather the death of altruism."[13]

Watergate had just faded into the background (though its consequences are still very much with us) when the Iran-Contra

11. William H. Becker, "The 1960s and Today's Vision of America," *Christian Century,* 29 May 1985, p. 559.

12. W. D. Ehrhart, *Vietnam-Perkasie: A Combat Marine Memoir* (Jefferson, NC: McFarland & Co., 1983), p. 305.

13. Levine, p. 137.

scandal was brought to the nation's attention. Once again a president and his aides were seen as coveting their own point of view in disregard of the spirit of the law, if not the law itself. According to the polls, the majority of Americans believe that the president had more to do with this event than he publicly admitted. However, perhaps not wanting to go through another Watergate, the American public seemed to absolve the president. Or is it that Americans after Vietnam and Watergate are willing to accept leadership that is less than truthful and that falls short of integrity? Is this a case where image has taken the place of truth, a phenomenon which seems to be the product of television? Or has America's pessimism and cynicism gone so far as to lower the country's expectations of its leadership?

Economic changes during the last part of this century have also contributed to self-doubt and pessimism in America.

During the first two-thirds of this century, the American economy was generally strong, despite the economic depression of the 1930s. Many Americans experienced a significant increase in their standard of living because of economic output and growth, particularly between 1930 and 1960. Robert Heilbroner observes of the American economy during this period that "such a condition of mass economic independence had never before characterized any large society."[14] This rise in standard of living came about as a result of economic output and growth.

The seventies and eighties have been quite a contrast. Two serious recessions plus high levels of inflation have plagued these two decades. But the most important economic factors in the past decades have been the decline of America's industrial productivity, the rise of the industrial growth and output of other countries, the buildup of a huge national debt, and a stubborn trade deficit of threatening proportions. The great American industrial spirit of confidence has disappeared. We now look with awe upon the productive power of Japan and other countries. We seem helpless to solve our industrial and therefore our economic problems. Self-doubt has America in its grip.

14. Heilbroner, *Future as History,* p. 127.

Self-doubt, the loss of idealism and our position as moral leaders in the world coupled with our lack of trustworthy national leadership, our economic decline within the world community—in addition to the ever-present threat of nuclear disaster, either through war or by accident—all of these factors have led to a totally new climate in America, a loss of hope in the future, at least among the nation's youth.

Before we consider this change in America's attitude toward the future, however, it is important that we examine how mankind has viewed time in the past.

Throughout most of human history, mankind focused on the past and present much more than on the future. Social institutions were oriented toward revering the past, honoring ancestors, and understanding life as mediated through those who had gone before. Human society was too preoccupied simply with survival to understand the forces of nature. Because of this a concept of human betterment and an ability to shape the future was almost nonexistent. Consequently, there was no undergirding philosophy of optimism about the future. This is something recent in human history. As Robert Heilbroner points out, "What was so egregiously lacking in this estimate of the future was a central conception of modern life: the idea of social movement, of aggregate betterment, of progress."[15] Heilbroner lists what needed to happen before our modern optimistic view of the future could develop:

> First, there was needed the power to alter man's subservience before nature to a mastery of it. Second, there was required a belief in the legitimacy of the idea of human betterment. And last there was missing a framework of social institutions which would combine power and hope, and which would then permit this fruitful combination to achieve its own spontaneous growth.[16]

An optimistic philosophy is almost exclusively an American phenomenon. As Robert Heilbroner points out, in earlier

15. *Ibid.*, p. 21.
16. *Ibid.*

history life had been "formidable and overwhelming, unaltera-ble and often unanswerable."[17] Optimism about the future is a uniquely American trait; this is why Americans are seen as brash and overconfident by people of other countries. Ameri-cans have not understood how unique their outlook on life actually is.

American optimism is the result of a number of factors, but surely one source is the Enlightenment. The English and French revolutions brought with them a sense of progress and hope in the political order. The technology brought about by the In-dustrial Revolution saw unheard-of technology applied success-fully to the daily life of most citizens. The rise of the middle class meant relative wealth and a high standard of living for masses of people. And in America this was played out with relatively little opposition in a vast and rich land. The massive participation in the benefits of this land itself became a dynamic force in Amer-ica. Heilbroner observes that

> No longer was it the large-scale individual acts of rulers that pro-vided the "force" of these new currents of social change, but rather the small-scale actions of thousands or even millions of human beings, integrating themselves into an anonymous agency of so-cial change. . . . At bottom it was the spread of political ideas from mind to mind, of economic pressure from market to market, of scientific advance from laboratory to laboratory which provided the metabolism of social growth and change.[18]

The sense of understanding and control which Americans developed vis-à-vis the natural order carried over to the social order. As we began to view the natural realm as orderly and therefore predictable, so the social realm seemed to be orderly and therefore predictable. American optimism reached its peak when we believed that both the natural order and the social order were controllable and predictable. Our ability to control and predict gave us a previously unheard-of sense of optimism

17. *Ibid.,* p. 18.
18. *Ibid.,* p. 29.

about the future. Progress was thought inevitable. Americans came to have so much self-confidence because they believed that the natural and social forces in the universe *and their particular chosen goals for the future* were not only compatible, but complementary!

But that sense of optimism was quickly lost during the 1970s. Instead of optimism, there was fear. Instead of self-confidence, there was self-doubt. Arthur Levine describes the results in the college students of the seventies: "There is a sense among today's undergraduates that they are passengers on a sinking ship, a Titanic if you will, called the United States or the world. Perhaps this is . . . why suicide has become the second leading cause of death among students in the 1970s, exceeded only by accidents."[19]

Social researcher Joseph Veroff and his colleagues, in studying the changes in American attitudes from the mid-fifties to the mid-seventies, found that optimism in America had dropped sharply during those two decades, that the future was no longer a concept that individuals saw as compatible with their well-being. Americans seemed to have discarded the future as something on which they could build their lives. Lacking a clear future to which they could direct their lives, young people in the mid-seventies experienced a great deal more anxiety. Then Veroff comments: "Uncertainty is a psychological problem that has many consequences."[20]

The new self-doubt in Americans seems to result, in part, from the fact that we are unable to exert any control over social forces, e.g., the threat of nuclear war and the continuation of the arms race, the change in the world economy and slippage in the American standard of living, guerrilla warfare and terrorism, and growing bureaucracy throughout life. As Heilbroner observes, "History less and less presents itself as something we *make*, and more and more as something we find made for us."[21]

19. Levine, pp. 104-5.

20. Joseph Veroff, Elizabeth Douvan, and Richard A. Kulk, *The Inner American: A Self-Portrait from 1957-1976* (New York: Basic Books, 1981), p. 528.

21. Heilbroner, *Future as History,* p. 55.

13

We are no longer masters as we had come to believe, but often feel as if we are slaves or objects. The change in outlook is so fast, and the significance so far-reaching, that it feels to many Americans as if the ground is crumbling beneath their feet in some seismic catastrophe.

This despair is new. We have not gone back to the historic view of our ancestors, namely, that of using the past to guide us in the present, but rather we have abandoned the past as worthless, inappropriate in these radically new times, as of no help in a new age.

Having lost the future and the past, more and more Americans, old and young alike, are focusing almost exclusively upon the present. Ours is no longer a society oriented to the future, but to the present.

This is the conclusion which college students had reached by the close of the seventies. The students of the eighties, having seen only further evidence that the future is unreliable, have continued in that same direction and as a result have been called "the me generation."

Ingrid Canright, a 1985 graduate, describes the students of the eighties. "Self-preoccupation in modern young people arises not so much from complacency as from desperation; it has become the faith of those without faith."[22] Unable to believe in the future and seemingly disconnected from the past, the students of the eighties have turned inward toward themselves as individuals. A new form of Epicureanism has emerged.

The Change in Value Systems and Morality

This pessimism and self-doubt which took hold in America in the seventies had a profound effect upon the value system and morality of many Americans. Alexis de Tocqueville, some 150 years ago, uttered a warning about the individualism that might emerge from the concepts of equality and democracy. He pre-

22. Canright, p. 72.

dicted that the elevation of the individual through democracy could lead to isolation and individualism. And his fears have now come true in America, though for slightly different reasons than he predicted:

> They owe nothing to any man, they expect nothing from any man; they acquire the habit of always considering themselves as standing alone, and they are apt to imagine that their whole destiny is in their own hands. Thus not only does democracy make every man forget his ancestors, but it hides his descendants and separates his contemporaries from him; it throws him back forever upon himself alone and threatens in the end to confine him entirely within the solitude of his own heart.[23]

Tocqueville had trusted that the family, religious traditions, and what he called "voluntary associations" would ameliorate the effects of individualism. In recent decades we have witnessed the weakening of all three of these potential support systems. The result has been pervasive individualism within American society.

Robert Bellah has pointed out that American life has become segregated, that it lacks integration. He states: "We have failed to remember 'our community as members of the same body,' as John Winthrop put it. We have committed what to the republican founders of our nation was the cardinal sin: we have put our own good, as individuals, as groups, as a nation, ahead of the common good."[24] Bellah laments the fact that individuals no longer participate in the larger moral ecology which would tie them to others. Instead, the individual finds a few persons of her own type to join her in pursuing a certain "life-style." The term "life-style" connotes very little, if any, commitment; rather, it demands only that persons have in common a similar age, salary level, type of job, and hobbies. It is a feeble attempt to curb the isolation and loneliness that result from individualism. However, it robs the individual of any deep commitment and last-

---

23. Alexis de Tocqueville, *Democracy In America,* vol. 2 (New York: Vintage Books, 1945), pp. 105-6.

24. Robert M. Bellah, Richard Madsen, William M. Sullivan, Ann Swidler, Steven M. Tipton, *Habits of the Heart* (New York: Harper & Row, 1985), p. 285.

ing friendships. Within the individualistic approach to life, the individual is "the only firm reality."[25]

The new word in American society is "relationship." The use of this word is ubiquitous. Some people can be heard using the word with relish. They use it to describe what in earlier decades would have been called a friendship, something implying commitment. But with individualism, friendship is no longer deep or lasting; it has no permanent commitment. The individual must be prepared to break out of connections with others if one's needs are not met. "Relationship" implies a friendship that can start and stop quickly and which involves little or no commitment.

Having become accomplished at relationships, Americans have transferred the concept to marriage. For many Americans, marriage is a form of relationship. There is only a modest increase in the amount of commitment in many contemporary marriages from that in nonmarital relationships. Relationships have become the model for marriage. One of Bellah's interviewees comments: "If other people don't meet your needs, you have to be willing to walk out, since in the end that may well be the only way to protect your interests."[26] Contemporary Americans feel free to walk out of marriage since it is only one form of relationship, and relationships by definition must be self-fulfilling or they should be abandoned.

Individualism is as hard on community life as it is on the life of our nation and our world. Persons who live for themselves feel no sense of responsibility for others around them. In contrast to the idealism of the sixties, when Americans set out to change their society through the Civil Rights Movement, and their world through the Peace Corps, today most Americans heed no such higher call, but instead devote their full time and attention to themselves.

But it is not only others who are hurt by individualism. The individual herself or himself is impoverished as well. Lacking in-

25. *Ibid.,* p. 276.
26. *Ibid.,* p. 16.

timate contact with persons who are unlike themselves, people living by the principles of individualism rob themselves of the richness of diversity found in a cross section of society by preferring persons who share their own "life-style." Unwilling to bear the cost of love, these persons do not experience the reward of loving and being loved. Worried about her own generation, Ingrid Canright, a graduate of the eighties, writes, "Love, like other commitments, takes a great deal of courage and work and the acceptance of a certain amount of risk. The premise is that it's worth it. I hope ultimately we decide it is."[27] Those who are unwilling to risk love and commitment will be left in the poverty of individualism. Involved in relationships which lack the element of commitment, the individual is constantly threatened by the loss of a "significant other," since commitment is not a part of "relationship." Fearing the possibility of loss makes such people hesitant and shallow. The individual is the poorer. Thus, what appears to be aimed at the well-being of the individual works only to his detriment.

In recent decades we have come to talk about "psychological man." Such words as "self-directedness," "self-expression," and "self-fulfillment," to name only a few, all point to the new emphasis upon the individual. Veroff and his fellow researchers point out that between the fifties and the seventies, men and women have become much more psychological in their thinking about themselves. People belong to fewer organizations now than they did in earlier decades, and they define themselves less on the basis of such organizations. Instead, they turn to a few select individuals for such self-definition. In the same vein, contemporary Americans look less to marriage as the source of well-being and focus more on their own personal characteristics and experiences as the source of their happiness. But while it might seem this focus on the self would increase happiness, Veroff points out that the opposite is true. The individual is constantly needing to verify himself, putting the burden of proof upon himself. The result is an individual's constant need to perform and to

27. Canright, p. 72.

achieve. Pressure exists even in relationships, because such relationships can and will be broken by others if the individual does not live up to the implied requirements of the relationship. Thus individualism leaves the person isolated, alone, and in constant need of proving himself.

Ingrid Canright urges her generation to overcome the fear of commitment.

> Whether or not we can overcome our fear is important not only to us individually, but also to the future of society. Yes, I hear their cynical laughter. But what kind of nation will we be if we cannot even commit ourselves to other people, much less to a set of abstract values? What kinds of families can we have if we cannot tolerate interdependence? What kinds of people will we be if we equate attachment with failure, autonomy—at any price—with strength? What kinds of politicians will we elect if self-interest is our highest value, humanity an "inoperative" commodity? Or have we already answered those questions?[28]

America's move to individualism has caused a profound shift in the basis of morality. Robert Bellah describes this change: "Feeling good oneself now stands in opposition to 'being good.'"[29] The person who lives on the basis of individualism gives up the traditional transcendent morality of the Judeo-Christian tradition, and in its place she establishes her own well-being as the basis of her actions. As "Margaret," one of Bellah's interviewees, says, "'I tend to operate on the assumption that what I want to do and what I feel like is what I should do. What I think the universe wants from me is to take my values, whatever they might happen to be, and live up to them as much as I can.'"[30] Bellah correctly observes that for the person living by individualism, "the right act is simply the one that yields the agent the most exciting challenge or the most good feeling about himself."[31] Each person constitutes her own moral universe. Each person relies

28. *Ibid.*
29. Bellah, p. 78.
30. *Ibid.*, p. 14.
31. *Ibid.*, p. 76.

upon her own feelings as a moral guide. "Acts, then, are not right or wrong in themselves, but only because of the results they produce, the good feelings they engender or express."[32]

This approach to morality has deep and widespread implications for a society in which individualism is rampant; indeed, the morality of such a society is at risk. There can be no common morality, but only many islands of morality created by individuals within that society. Veroff speaks of this profound shift in the basis of morality as a shift from a "moral orientation" to a "psychological orientation," and indicates that there was a significant movement in this direction in America from the mid-1950s to the mid-1970s.[33] Arthur Levine observed this same movement in personal freedom—the right of individuals to pursue their own lives without the encumbrance of external restrictions.[34] This is also one of the major points of Allan Bloom. The term he applies to it is "relativism." Bloom writes that "there is one thing a professor can be absolutely certain of: almost every student entering the university believes, or says he believes, that truth is relative. . . . The relativity of truth is not a theoretical insight but a moral postulate, the condition of a free society, or so they see it. . . . There are no absolutes; freedom is absolute."[35]

America's shift in morality has been aided and abetted by television and by advertising. The American economy is not based upon the *needs* or the *necessities* of life. Appealing to a sense of need that is created within individuals by advertising, our economy is based on desire, advertising-created desire, rather than on need. Here is a very subtle shift in the concept of truth or fact in our society. Perceptions replace facts; feelings replace facts. As a result, not only have we given up the concept of truthfulness in our society, but we have also thereby increased public cynicism. Political campaigns, particularly those relying heavily upon television, have shifted to using the techniques of advertis-

32. *Ibid.*, p. 78.
33. Veroff, Douvan, and Kulk, pp. 25, 28.
34. Levine, p. 85.
35. Allan Bloom, *The Closing of the American Mind: Education and the Crisis of Reason* (New York: Simon and Schuster, 1987), pp. 25, 28.

ing, and in so doing they have moved from truth-telling to image-making. We have become a nation which bases its political choices on images, perceptions which we know may not be the same as the truth. This only feeds the growth of cynicism within a citizenry.

A similar shift can be seen in the use of language within our society. New words are coined in order to fill them with the meaning a person wants these words to convey, often in exchange for words which would convey the truth. We have seen this done by government spokespersons. We have come to expect the distortion of facts from our government. As a result, we are left to our own devices to figure out for ourselves what the truth is.

The rapid growth of science and technology is also having a profound impact upon contemporary Americans. The original goal of the Industrial Revolution was the elevation of the human condition, and advances in medicine particularly have contributed to this goal. This has happened particularly in the field of medicine. But we may have reached the point of diminishing returns. The current technology which is breaking upon the scene, a largely electronic technology, may be lowering the quality of life as it speeds up the tempo and forces its own control over its users. In tandem with growing bureaucracy, the new electronic technology is having a profound effect upon the entire citizenry. The complexity of life resulting from these two forces diminishes the human spirit; many persons experience a feeling of sinking importance.

For all the good that it has done, science and technology have also eroded the human spirit. Robert Heilbroner describes the society which science and technology has created. "This 'society' is not the interplay of intimates, but the impersonal articulation of millions of strangers into a working whole. It is the creation of an environment in which human beings 'function' as parts of an elaborate social machine, and in which there are ever fewer aspects of life which do not involve the cooperative effort of other human beings. . . . Thus we find that the incursion of science and technology creates an ever-higher order of *social control*."[36] The

36. Heilbroner, *Future as History,* pp. 73-74.

increasing social control of science and technology has led us to feel that we have lost control over our environment and habitat. Earlier Americans were able to overcome their feelings of helplessness and lack of control of their environment, and this led to their optimism and self-confidence. Will we be able to do the same, or will science and technology ultimately lead us back to the age-old condition of mankind where man has no sense of the future—this time not as the result of nature, but as the result of human inventions?

A CRISIS IN DIRECTION AND MEANING IN NATION AND INDIVIDUAL

Whether it is due to growing secularity, to the new pluralism which marks the American landscape, to the individualism which has invaded the American spirit, or to some combination of these and other factors, a lack of moral direction and meaning affects the lives of many Americans, as well as the American nation as a whole.

It has been easy for cynicism to permeate the population—particularly the youth—when the leadership at the very top of our nation for several decades has lacked moral integrity. While the reaction of many young people to this lack of moral integrity is wrong, it is understandable. To turn inward, to find one's own basis of morality, is a natural reaction. But this is a reaction that only further decays the moral fiber of our nation.

Joining governmental leaders in the lack of moral integrity are visible and powerful business leaders. For example, the practice of insider trading on Wall Street by people who are considered leaders of the business community is not a model that will give the proper direction to a nation searching for a national morality.

TV evangelists who publicly decry the immorality of others so vividly on the screen have themselves been caught up in the very behaviors they condemned. These evangelists have urged their viewers to reject "worldly society" in favor of an "other-worldly" life, only to find that they themselves have succumbed to that which they abhor. Many people in America feel let down, misled. And while the TV evangelists do not represent the whole church, they injure the entire church.

Thus the so-called "leadership" of the nation, whether in government, business, or the church, has not only failed to lead the nation toward a high standard of morality; they have misled a nation which sorely needs moral leadership.

Add to this the breakdown of the American family. Children and youth are not given the training and nurture they need. Many do not receive training in morality, nor are they shown how to live a life of moral integrity. Because of the breakdown of the family, many of society's institutions, including the public schools, are not able to build the moral fiber of the nation the way they should.

Perhaps America's drug problem is the clearest expression of our problem. The federal government attempts to solve the drug problem by focusing not on the millions of drug users in this country but on the foreign nations which produce and distribute drugs. It must appear to federal officials that it is easier to eradicate the world's production of drugs than to try to bring enough direction and meaning into the lives of Americans that they find drugs unnecessary. Something seems to be wrong, missing, at the core of many Americans' lives.

As I was writing this book in Princeton, New Jersey, the results of a survey on alcohol and drug use among eleventh grade students in the local high school was published in the newspaper. The survey was carried out by the Hazelden Foundation, a Minnesota-based organization proficient in the study of drug and alcohol abuse. The survey showed that almost three-fourths of the juniors had used alcohol during the month of March, 1987. Thirty-one percent had taken five or more drinks in a row during a two-week period in March. Thirty-one percent of the juniors had used marijuana during that month; four percent had used cocaine; eleven percent of the juniors had used hallucinogens.[37] What is particularly noteworthy is that these statistics are about young American

37. *Town Topics,* Vol. XLII, No. 29 (30 September 1987): 1.

high school juniors who come from the "best" homes and are students in one of the "best" school systems in the country. By all appearances, they have everything going for them. It seems that something has gone wrong in American society, that something is sadly lacking in the lives of these and many other American youth.

It is sad to admit that higher education has not provided a solution to this problem; indeed, it may be part of the cause. Derek Bok, president of Harvard University, told his Board of Overseers in the spring of 1988:

> Despite the importance of moral development to the individual student and the society, one cannot say that higher education has demonstrated a deep concern for the problem. . . . Universities will never do much to encourage a genuine concern for ethical issues or to help their students to acquire a strong and carefully considered set of moral values unless presidents and deans take the lead. . . .
>
> An equal responsibility rests with the faculty. . . . More than any other group, they set the tone of the institution, and establish what is important, what is legitimate, what truly merits the time and attention of the students. Unless professors recognize the importance of moral education, unless they personally participate by treating ethical issues in their classes, counseling students, helping to define and administer rules of behavior on campus, any effort along these lines will lack credibility and force. Indeed, without such involvement, scholarly traditions of value-free inquiry may foster a sense among students and administrators that ethical questions are private matters to be kept out of serious conversation. . . .
>
> One can appreciate the difficulty of the task and understand if progress is slow and halting. What is harder to forgive is a refusal to recognize the problem or to acknowledge a responsibility to work at it conscientiously.[38]

For too many decades, higher education has washed its hands of assisting individuals and the nation with developing moral integrity. The result is that the leadership of this nation has lacked moral integrity.

38. Derek Bok, *The Chronicle of Higher Education*, 27 April 1988, p. B4.

2. Mainline Protestant Churches in the Post–World War II Years

To tell the story of the mainline Protestant churches in America after World War II without first creating a context will distort the picture and mislead the reader. The decade of the fifties did not just happen. However, time allows only a few brief comments before we launch into the 1950s.

Martin Marty points out that historians—and, I presume, the average citizen as well—should not have been surprised that the decades following the Second World War saw the decline of the mainline Protestant churches in America because "after the 1730s, the mainline was almost always in retreat, always being overtaken by new competing forces."[1] There was a powerful connection between the early Protestant colonialists and the American government. The influence in American society by people whose religious persuasion was mainline Protestant was larger than life. But that influence from the start and for three hundred years has been diluted by the beliefs and traditions of wave after wave of immigrants populating America. Little wonder that the views of new American citizens should finally take their place in the land. The wonder is not so much the decline as the staying power of the mainline Protestant denominations in American society.

1. Martin E. Marty, *Religion and Republic: The American Circumstance* (Boston: Beacon Press, 1987), p. 331.

So though our awareness of American pluralism may be new, pluralism itself is not. Mainline Protestant power has only kept at bay the implications of that pluralism. Time was on the side of pluralism, and after World War II the scale began to tip its way.

The 1950s didn't reflect that trend, but that decade was an anomaly. The fifties saw an amazing recovery in mainline churches, but it was a positive blip on an otherwise downward trend. We should not view the fifties as the norm or be surprised today with the continued decline.

With that brief background, let us look at each decade, beginning with the 1950s.

THE DECADE OF THE 1950S

In many ways the decade of the fifties was a replay of the glory days of the 1920s. Affluence, self-confidence, and a healthy economy were characteristics of America, but they were also the characteristics of mainline Protestantism. In the 1940s, life had been uprooted by the Second World War. When the soldiers came home they wanted to settle down and establish families. The mainline Protestant denominations provided the ambience for doing that. Young parents reached back into their childhood years of Sunday school and church attendance and attempted to resume their lives where they had left off prior to the war. In many ways President Eisenhower was the model for faith and life. Higher education helped countless numbers of veterans establish themselves in the burgeoning middle class. As churches of the middle class, the mainline Protestant denominations benefited from the veterans' search for respectability and stability.

The veterans flocked to the suburbs in an attempt to secure the pastoral life which they so earnestly sought. The result was twofold. First, it brought about an unprecedented level of church building as the mainline denominations followed their population to the suburbs. Never before in American history had citizens been spending proportionately as much per year on church building and never before had a higher percentage of people been on church rolls. Attendance and monetary giving reached new highs. Second, as mainline Protestantism moved to the suburbs, theological differences became less important than they had been throughout history. Instead of focusing on their past theological identities, the mainline denominations downplayed their theological traditions and differences. The wide acceptance of Billy Graham demonstrated how theologically inclusive the mainline Protestant churches had become. Theological differences were eclipsed in an attempt by mainline Protestant churches to attract the suburbanites to their churches. The new focus was on providing fellowship for those who lived far away from their extended families as a result of the new mobility in America, and who were therefore in need of new means of connecting with others.

Church architecture followed suit. As a part of the new focus on attracting new members, the suburban mainline Protestant churches attempted to make people feel welcome through their architecture, with low entrances and new seating patterns; instead of sitting in rows before the pulpit to hear the authoritative word of God, these churches had people sitting "in the round" with the communion table in the middle. (More will be said in a later chapter about church architecture.) While the theology and architecture were acceptable, these changes did involve a distinct shift in emphasis. Lost was the sense of God's authority; in its place was the welcoming presence of the people of God. It should not surprise us that in the 1950s God was often seen as a benevolent, if benign, "man upstairs," rather than the traditional God of dominion.

Standards for church membership declined, and as they did church membership rose, particularly in the mainline Protestant denominations. When membership crested, 64 percent of American citizens were church members and 50 percent of American citizens claimed to be attending worship each week.[2] An evan-

2. Martin E. Marty, *Righteous Empire: The Protestant Experience in America* (New York: Dial Press, 1970), p. 259.

gelical fervor throughout much of mainline Protestantism re-
kindled the fires of belief in "manifest destiny." The popularity of
prayer breakfasts in Washington, D.C., gave the populace the
feeling that things were right in America. America was riding
high; mainline Protestantism was riding high.

Reinhold Niebuhr was one of only a few theologians who
was uncomfortable in the 1950s. He believed that mainline Protestantism was too comfortable, too tied into "the American Way
of Life." Reinhold and his brother, H. Richard Niebuhr, believed
that mainline Protestants, not to mention the evangelicals and
fundamentalists, were not hearing—let alone meeting—the
needs of a hurting world. Americans, both Niebuhrs claimed,
were too self-centered. But, comments Martin Marty, "during the
Eisenhower years, the people were not ready for that message.
Not until American goals faded in the 1960s, especially with the
Vietnamese War, did such realism make its point."[3]

THE DECADE OF THE 1960s

Then came the decade of the 1960s. If the 1950s were an understandable anomaly, the 1960s were a puzzling anomaly. This decade too must be viewed in its proper context. We have already
seen part of that context—the fifties—as a throwback to the
twenties. In both the twenties and fifties Americans were pro-
cessing the effects of a world war. Everyone wanted to have a
good world and a good life after each of these wars. But the fifties were not enough of a context for the sixties. Earlier decades
played their role. The wave of immigrants may have found a new
life in America, but their lives were shaped by the established
power which did not always accord them full citizenship. This
tension of inequity had been building, as had the one that left
blacks as second-class citizens. For centuries Americans had
dreamt and talked about a just world, a just America. But the

3. Marty, *Pilgrims in Their Own Land* (New York: Penguin Books, 1985),
p. 417.

awareness in the sixties, says Sydney Alstrom, was "of vast contradictions in American life between profession and performance, the ideal and the actual" along with "increasing doubt as to the capacity of . . . ecclesiastical, political, social and educational institutions to rectify the country's deep-seated woes," in addition to "a growing commitment to a naturalism or secularism and corresponding doubts about the supernatural and the sacral."[4] In short, many pent-up issues that had been building for years exploded in the sixties. Intellectually aware of these issues, Sydney Ahlstrom speaks from the heart when he poses the question: "Why . . . did so many diverse processes drop their bomb load on the sixties?"[5]

During the 1960s, Americans, including mainline Protestants, attempted to handle these diverse yet interrelated issues. The radical theologians, including the death-of-God proponents, attempted to handle our changing understanding of God and the natural world which had begun with Copernicus, Galileo, and Newton. Advances in the biological sciences since Charles Darwin called into question the nature of man's origin as Scripture tells it, as well as the biblical and popular idea of creation. Freud and a host of other psychologists and psychiatrists raised haunting questions about the inner workings of the human mind and soul. Einstein, much to his chagrin, was misunderstood by many people to suggest that we live in a relativistic world; thus many felt justified in developing a relativistic ethic in place of traditional authority. War was raising questions about the relationship between God, history, and America's place in the scheme of things. Modern technology was raising questions about man's place in the scheme of the universe, doubts fueled by growing bureaucracy. The urban explosion raised doubts about the value of the historic pastoral way of life and the traditional American values associated with rural life.

Ahlstrom suggests that these powerful forces might have

4. Sydney E. Ahlstrom, *A Religious History of the American People* (New Haven: Yale University Press, 1972), p. 1087.
5. *Ibid.*

been handleable had it not been for additional forces that converged at that particular time. Unregulated urban and industrial growth created social conditions with which American political and fiscal practices could not cope. Migrations of people changed voting patterns and affected key decisions by the Supreme Court; technology fostered an inability to develop a workable understanding of transcendence; the development and use of the bomb and the subsequent arms race raised doubts about the future of the human race; and finally, the Vietnam War escalated, with a subsequent loss by Americans in their nation's credibility.[6] As Ahlstrom concludes, "one may safely say that America's moral and religious tradition was tested and found wanting in the sixties."[7]

Ahlstrom cites varying reactions to the tumultuous 1960s. It seemed to some that the time-honored structures of the American church were irrelevant. The church attendance of the 1950s seemed to some more like an obstacle to change; therefore, in the sixties it fell off. Education, instead of leading to a good society, seemed to be leading the country's youth to turn against church and society. To many people, evidence of God's love was hard to find, in contrast to the 1950s. Racism was exposed for all to see. Part of the population wondered if a just society could ever be achieved, while another part wanted to install leaders who would reestablish law and order. Militancy turned out to frighten young and old alike, and it was counterproductive. Radical theology tried to resonate with people in their despair. Most people concluded that America was not the "chosen country" that other generations believed it was. Finally, hopelessness crept into the souls of many following the tragic assassinations of some of America's leaders.[8]

The 1960s were indeed a time of turmoil in America, a disturbing time when America looked deeply into her soul and did not like all that she saw. As Martin Marty observes: "Energies

6. *Ibid.,* pp. 1091-93.
7. *Ibid.,* p. 1085.
8. *Ibid.,* pp. 1093-94.

devoted to building up one day were directed to tearing down the next. Devotion to religious institutions in one decade became massive assault on religious institutionalism in the next."[9]

To their credit, the mainline Protestant denominations were in the thick of the struggle. Outspoken clergy and laypersons alike gave support to the Civil Rights Movement and visible resistance to the Vietnam War. But that kind of leadership sometimes proved to be costly: many clergy and laity did not welcome such leadership on those issues. An age-old split reemerged between those who believed the gospel called them to change the world and those who believed that such social action was not in the domain of the church.

The late sixties were characterized by conflict: conflict within the mainline Protestant churches, within the nation, and between these churches and the nation. In Martin Marty's words, "The late 1960s saw Americans in conflict as seldom before: men versus women, young people versus their elders, leftists versus right-wingers, hawks versus doves, blacks versus whites, homosexuals versus straights, hippies versus squares, Eastern religionists versus conventional congregants, countercultural Aquarians against nostalgic upholders of the olden ways—these all conspired to show how diverse and restless, how unsettled Americans were."[10]

THE DECADE OF THE 1970S

After the turbulent 1960s came the 1970s, a decade of reactions to the 1960s. As Ahlstrom puts it, "dissensus was more visible than consensus"[11] during these years.

Some Americans—the "hippies" and "flower children," for example—chose to drop out, deliberately spurning traditional society and its values through their actions. They saw communal

9. Marty, *Righteous Empire*, p. 255.
10. Marty, *Pilgrims*, pp. 429-30.
11. Ahlstrom, p. 1093.

living as an alternative—living by a whole new set of values with less emphasis upon competition and individualism and more emphasis upon cooperation and community.

The students of the 1970s showed far less interest in social action than had students in the sixties. An incredible amount of cynicism toward government permeated the American citizenry, but especially affected the youth. The shootings at Kent State University, the Vietnam War, and Watergate all fed this cynicism. The energy and environmental crises often seemed insurmountable. Instead, students began to focus on themselves and their individual futures. A severe recession in the 1970s encouraged students to focus on their education and on preparing for a job. Thus, whereas students of the sixties focused on their society, students of the seventies focused on their own well-being.

As far as religion was concerned, the 1960s had broken the spell on American society of mainline Protestant values and power. After the sixties America was clearly a pluralistic society. In addition to what came to be called "WASPS," many other Americans from a wide variety of religious, cultural, and ethnic backgrounds would now have their place in American society. Martin Marty points out that instead of disappearing after it had taken such a beating in the 1960s, religion relocated. Religious expression became more private, personal, and eclectic. It was far less tied to organizations and institutions. The move of the masses was toward the privatization of religion in the wake of social involvement in the 1960s.

If religious life was still vital in the 1970s, it did take on some different forms and appearances. While some people dropped out, others joined a growing number of cults in an attempt to find the spirituality and authority they were missing in mainline Protestantism.

Many individuals and groups focused on the "interior journey" of faith. Often such journeys used primitive images to contend with the complexities of modern life. "They wanted to go back: to nature, to the primitives, to the American Indians, to Catholic authority, to Africa, to the Bible, to the old family album of old-time religion, to the experience of being born again, and even back spiritually to the Asian continent."[12] The religious landscape of America had changed radically between the 1950s and the 1970s.

Strangely enough, civil religion grew in the 1970s. After the beating that political and religious institutions took in the 1960s, it seems surprising that civil religion recovered so soon. But recover it did. "A succession of presidents before and after the bicentennial in 1976 waved the flag that Ahlstrom and others had last seen desecrated in radical protest movements. By the time of Ronald Reagan's presidency in the 1980s, there were sounds from the White House of the old language of American righteousness over against its enemies, notably the Soviet 'evil empire.' The call for 'traditional values' was widespread as, in reaction to turbulence and pluralism, many Americans invoked images of the simpler days."[13] Civil religion was taking its place among other religious expressions during the 1970s.

The clear losers in the 1970s—in both numbers and influence—were the mainline Protestant denominations. While the mainline Protestant denominations had grown considerably in the 1950s and early 1960s, they experienced sharp losses from the middle of the 1960s through the 1970s and into the 1980s. Jackson Carroll and his fellow researchers show that in these mainline Protestant denominations, church membership was down, church attendance was down, church giving declined, and religious influence decreased.[14]

Strikingly, the decline was greatest among people under age 30.[15] The mainline Protestant denominations experienced the defection of many of their youth, leaving many of these churches without the idealism and energy of youth, but also leaving these young people to drift into secularism, without any formal religious orientation and no sense of the transcendent.

12. Marty, *Pilgrims*, p. 437.

13. Martin E. Marty, *Protestantism in the United States: Righteous Empire*, 2d ed. (New York: Charles Scribner's Sons, 1986), p. 258.

14. Jackson W. Carroll et al. *Religion in America: 1950 to the Present* (San Francisco: Harper & Row, 1979), pp. 22-23.

15. *Ibid.*, p. 32.

It is important to trace carefully the causes of this membership decline in the mainline Protestant denominations. Many have simply attributed all of the loss to the deep involvement of these denominations in the social causes of the 1960s. Indeed, for some this involvement was cause enough to defect from their denominations. Carroll makes two significant points in this regard:

> First, there was considerable negative reaction from the denominational constituencies to those activities that were highly visible and widely publicized. . . . Second . . . by the beginning of the 1960s, one after another criticism began to be leveled at the churches for their "sell-out" to the "number and success game," and for their irrelevance in the urban crisis and the struggle for racial justice. Responding to these emerging social issues and to the criticisms, denominational leaders shifted priorities. Among the major changes of the liberal denominations was a shift from new church development to the programs of social and economic justice mentioned above. . . .Thus the shift in priorities away from new church development to support of social concerns seems to be an important factor in understanding trends in membership and participation during the 1960s. We are not criticizing here the shift in priorities. Rather, our concern is to point out that membership losses in many denominations during the 1960s were more likely a result of the shift in priorities than of a wholesale defection in protest to social action. Had the churches been able to manage both social activism and new church development, the declines might not have been so severe.[16]

Other factors have insured the continued loss of membership, vitality, and influence of the mainline Protestant denominations into the eighties. The decline of young people in these churches is partly the result of a change in birthrate trends among the members of these denominations. Instead of having four or five children as they did in the 1950s, families in recent decades are more likely to have one or two children, some no children at all. In addition, many children of mainline Protestant families

16. *Ibid.*, p. 41.

began to reject some of the values held by their parents. Indeed, cynicism about these earlier values helped shape the new movement toward emphasis on the self. Personal fulfillment replaced social change as the goal of these young people. Issues of freedom, autonomy, and tolerance—which form the current agenda of youth—were not particularly concerns of the mainline Protestant denominations. It is somewhat ironic that, whereas American youth in the sixties were deeply concerned about and involved with social causes, the youth of the seventies and eighties abandoned such concerns and lost touch with those denominations which attempted to pursue social concerns. The agenda of the mainline Protestant churches in the 1970s did not match the agenda of American youth.

There are additional reasons why the mainline churches lost membership and influence. One has to do with demographics, such as population shifts. The Northeast and Midwest sections of the country—largely urban areas—began to experience a sharp decline in population as a result of economic decline. This area came to be called the "Rustbelt." In contrast, the southern tier of states, called the "Sunbelt," experienced sharp growth. The mainline Protestant denominations had been located largely in the northeast and midwest states and thus these churches suffered from the area's economic and population decline. By the same token, the evangelical churches were located in the southern states, and therefore the evangelical churches stood to gain in the demographic shift.[17]

Still another reason for the decline in the mainline Protestant denominations had to do with the de-emphasis of certain doctrines. The mainline Protestant denominations had become friendly with groups with whom they were once adversaries. The ecumenical spirit in the mainline denominations encouraged them to seek union with some of these groups. As a result, the mainline Protestant denominations downplayed those doctrines and unique features which would obstruct ecumenism.They "favored low, figurative walls and weak boundaries. They did not

17. *Ibid.*, pp. 38-42.

provide people with clear identities."[18] This loss of doctrinal authority and other unique features played into the hands of the evangelical churches who emphasized unique identities. To many Americans, the mainline Protestant denominations had accommodated too much to an increasingly secular society. Martin Marty observes: "In an age that encouraged exclusiveness to promote identity, the mainline was not particular enough about boundaries and offered less sense of belonging than did rigid groups. In a period of new fanaticism, it tried to stay civil and non-aggressive. In a time when personal experience received the highest premium, the older established churches remained somewhat staid and diffident about promoting 'peak experiences' and getting people to talk about them."[19]

The mainline Protestant denominations found themselves in a conundrum in the 1970s. To many people, particularly those who favored a more evangelical approach to the Christian faith, the mainline Protestant denominations seemed to have given in to secularity, partly by trying to come to grips with some of the contemporary radical theologies. This might have given the mainline Protestant denominations a distinct place in the religious spectrum in America. But the mainline Protestant denominations believe in transcendence, and this belief in transcendence puts them at odds with modern secularity even as they attempt to address it. It is not clear in the minds of many Americans just where mainline Protestant denominations stand vis-à-vis traditional Christian faith and modern secularity.

One additional development seems to trouble these denominations. In the 1960s, it was often the leadership of these denominations—clergy and lay—which drew these denominations into involvement in social causes. Therefore it is not surprising that these denominations adopted the principle of "affirmative action" in hiring church leadership, both to draw minorities into leadership and the mainstream of American life, and to be true to a commitment to affirmative action. Thus, women, blacks, and

---

18. Marty, *Protestantism,* pp. 260-61.
19. Marty, *Pilgrims,* p. 473.

Hispanics were placed in key leadership positions, replacing to some extent the all white, male leadership of the past. Several things resulted. First, this new leadership is unfamiliar to the membership of these denominations, and the growing bureaucracy doesn't encourage as intimate a knowledge of church leaders as was customary in years gone by. Second, as one might expect, their style of leadership is different from that of the white males. Third, those leaders who are from minority groups will have different agendas than the agendas of the previous white-male leadership. As a result, mainline Protestant denominations are experiencing the pain and confusion of change. To church members it seems as if the church is stuck on the agenda of social change. Other members are happy to see that social issues are still being addressed.

No description of the condition of the mainline Protestant denominations in the 1970s would be complete without noting the sharp rise of membership, church giving, and overall influence of the conservative churches in America. If the mainline Protestant denominations experienced decline, the conservative churches experienced growth.[20] It came as a surprise that, following the sixties, when vociferous voices spoke against the institutional church, we would have a succession of presidents in the United States who called themselves "born again" Christians; so quickly did American society change.

Martin Marty describes the factors that are contributing to the growth of the conservative churches:

> In many respects evangelicalism fits the pattern of all the movements of the 1970s. On one hand, it tended to give people a sense of belonging, of peoplehood: they acquired an identity. On the other, it put a high premium on what Robert Heilbroner called "inner states of experience," and was emotionally satisfying to people who could not do much to change the world of external fact around them. Evangelical leaders portrayed themselves as being in opposition to "the spirit of the times," though in many respects their success-minded movement played up to it. Whatever

20. Carroll, Johnson, and Marty, p. 37.

the fate of organized religion in America, the Protestant born-again movement was likely to keep at least its one-third share among the Christian majority for some time to come.[21]

Congressman John B. Anderson rather gleefully described to a meeting of conservative church people the reversal in the American church scene:

It was *they* (the liberals) who denied the supernatural acts of God, conforming the gospel to the canons of modern science. . . . It was *they* who found financial support for architectural monuments to their cause. It was *they* who were the friends of those in positions of political power. *They* were the "beautiful people," and *we*—you will recall—were the "kooks." We were regarded as rural, reactionary, illiterate fundamentalists who just didn't know better.

Well, things have changed. Now *they* are the "kooks"—and we are the "beautiful people." *Our* prayer breakfasts are so popular that only those with engraved invitations are allowed to attend. *Our* evangelists have the ready ear of those in positions of highest authority. Our churches are growing, and theirs are withering. . . . *They* are tired, worn-out, 19th-century liberals trying to repair the pieces of an optimism shattered by world wars, race riots, population explosion, and the spectre of worldwide famine.[22]

It is important to have a balanced view of the mainline Protestant denominations in the 1970s. True, there were those who were angry with their church, stopped attending, stopped contributing, or defected. There was confusion over what precisely these denominations stood for. The spirit which pervaded these denominations during the growth decade of the fifties and the very different spirit which pervaded them in the sixties were greatly diminished in the 1970s. They were no longer located in the best economic region of the country. Their youth were diminishing in number and seemed to be taking on the more self-centered and secular philosophy of life so prevalent in the 1970s.

21. Marty, *Pilgrims,* p. 473.
22. In James C. Hefley and Edward E. Plowman, *Washington: Christians in the Corridors of Power* (Wheaton, IL: Tyndale House, 1975), p. 195.

Yet there were also signs of vitality. The black churches, under the leadership of persons following in the footsteps of Martin Luther King, Jr., joined the mainstream of Protestant denominations and became much more of a force in the religious life of America, as well as in America's political scene.

A second new force, perhaps even a greater one in mainline Protestant denominations, was the women's movement, which went beyond the laity in its effects. By the late 1970s most Protestant denominations *ordained* women. The beginning of a complete face-change was underway in the mainline Protestant denominations. Marty writes of women in the church: "Numbers of them did come to be leaders of denominations, and they were highly visible agents in church conventions and task forces."[23] It is not a thing of insignificance that in the 1970s the mainline Protestant denominations broke through the two-thousand-year-old pattern of male dominance in the church.

The ecumenical movement in the mainline Protestant denominations which had begun in the 1950s and continued in the 1960s *seemed* to diminish in the 1970s. But a more careful look shows that, rather than focusing on ecumenical activity at the national level, much of the focus was on the local level. A spirit of divisiveness was being replaced at the local level by a spirit of cooperation; thus, one of the criticisms of the institutional church during the 1960s was being addressed in a very meaningful way in the 1970s.

Somewhat the same thing was true for social action. In retrospect, what seemed to bother some parishioners in the mainline Protestant denominations was not so much social action per se, but the highly vocal pronouncements and the highly visible activities at the national level. Rather than retreating from social action, the mainline Protestant denominations moved many of their social action activities to the local level. As Martin Marty points out, "If there was now less social action in the form of public demonstrations and passage of social justice resolutions, there were compensatory local expressions. Local churches developed

23. Marty, *Protestantism*, p. 260.

hospices and worked for better distribution of health care. Many welcomed 'boat people,' refugees from Southeast Asia, and took steps to improve care of the aged. They provided sanctuaries for Central American dissidents and participated in debates over nuclear armament."[24]

As we reflect on the seventies, there were clear signs of decline in the mainline Protestant denominations, but there were also these signs of vitality. Popularity should not be the only criterion of success or vitality. Doing the *right things* should also count. And it must be said that while the mainline Protestant denominations were doing some wrong things as well as leaving some things undone, they were also doing some right things. There was vitality and hope in the midst of decline.

THE DECADE OF THE 1980s

The 1980s have not had as clear an "identity" as has each of the preceding decades that we have discussed. In some ways the 1980s are a continuation of the 1970s. It may also be that we are too close to the 1980s to have a proper perspective.

Signs have indicated that the membership drop in the mainline Protestant denominations leveled off during the eighties, even though the shift in population from the Rustbelt to the Sunbelt did not.

There were no signs of a quickening of theology. The mainline Protestant denominations still seemed under the spell of Reinhold Niebuhr, the theologian of "Christian realism." Niebuhr's emphasis upon ethics to the exclusion of theology and liturgy took hold in the 1960s and continued into the 1980s. Niebuhr emphasized that the gospel must be applied to the nation as well as to the individual and therefore he was the architect of the emphasis upon social action. His disinterest in theology came to be an earmark of mainline Protestant theology from the sixties to today. The little theological focus present in mainline Protestantism

24. *Ibid.*, p. 261.

during the 1980s involved an attempt to come to grips with liberation theology and feminist theology.

Early in the 1980s, much of the energy of some mainline Protestant denominations was concentrated on decentralizing the church structure. The attempt to relate more closely to the average parishioner was made through various forms of decentralization. In the second half of the decade, some of the administrative headquarters of these denominations were relocated in order to be closer to the local church. An enormous amount of time, energy, and money was poured into these efforts. Only time will tell if they will be productive.

Martin Marty, in one of his most poignant remarks, points out that both in the religious revival years of the 1950s and in the social revolution years of the 1960s, spiritual concerns took a backseat in the mainline Protestant denominations. "Urgent issues of theology, ethics, and the social forms of the church had so preoccupied the elite and the avant-garde of the religious communities that they tended to ignore 'the spiritual dimension' of both individual and collective life."[25] Unfortunately, what started in the 1950s and carried through the 1960s has also been true of the 1970s and 1980s in the mainline Protestant denominations. Again, quoting Marty: "Once, spiritual man was seen to be the one who stood before the *mysterium tremendum*. He maintained a direct or clearly mediated access to a transcendent order or being."[26] Unfortunately, it seems that the mainline Protestant denominations' focus on ethics to the exclusion of theology and liturgics, and their focus on action instead of contemplation, has led to an unbalanced church life.

Another development, one which perhaps had been in the making since the 1960s but which came to be more and more evident in the 1980s, is the growing rift between the mainline Protestant denominations and the American government. More will be said about this topic in a later chapter. Suffice it to say now that for two centuries the mainline Protestant denomina-

25. Marty, *Religion and Republic*, p. 124.
26. *Ibid.*, p. 125.

tions had had a special relationship as allies of the federal government. Many government leaders—presidents, legislators, justices, and a host of governmental support staff—had been members of the mainline Protestant denominations. But that alliance has come undone; neither can assume the support of the other. Perhaps one cause underlying this development was America's shift from being the moral leader in the world to being the leader by virtue of its power—a shift that seems to have happened after the Second World War. Instead of the mainline Protestant denominations, the conservative churches are now aligned with the federal government.

Martin Marty declares that from the Second World War through the 1980s the mainline Protestant denominations misread three basic ingredients in the traditional religious life of Americans: first, a hunger for a personal religious experience; second, a need for authority in the face of growing relativism; and third, a need for religious institutions and movements that provide personal identity and help establish and maintain a sense of belonging and social location.[27] These deep-seated needs were being addressed by the conservative churches.

Most, if not all, of the mainline Protestant churches have these dimensions within their traditions. It remains to be seen if these dimensions can be resurrected and brought to new life in these churches. To Marty's three points I will add a fourth: that the Christian faith is more than ethics, though it includes ethics. There must be a personal, spiritual relationship with God, who is known in Jesus Christ. This faith must be exercised and refreshed through worship and Christian nurture *and* it must find expression in the life of the individual and in the life of our society and our world. This dimension is present in the traditions of the mainline Protestant denominations; it must find expression in these churches if they are to recover their spiritual energy and meet the spiritual needs of their parishioners.

27. *Ibid.,* p. 340.

3. Higher Education in America after World War II

Before we can understand the changes which took place in higher education in America after World War II, we must first be familiar with the history of higher education in America prior to World War II. A brief sketch of American higher education from colonial times to the Second World War will suffice.

The colonial colleges were founded very early in the life of the colonies. Harvard was founded in 1636, with William and Mary, Yale, King's College (Columbia University), Dartmouth, and Princeton following. A religious impulse lay behind the founding of most of the colonial colleges; even when the college was not directly affiliated with a denomination, the intentions of the founders was to enrich the moral and spiritual growth of the students along with their intellectual and cultural growth. Their purpose was twofold: first, to provide an educated clergy for the colonies, and second, to provide leadership through the other professions for the general well-being of the growing colonies. It wasn't long after the founding of these colleges that the colonies were able to rely upon their own institutions for leadership in the churches as well as in society.

The nature of these early colleges cannot be fully understood apart from the milieu in which they were founded and the cultural ambience which sustained them. That matters of faith would be addressed in these colleges was assumed. These colleges were founded by religious persons for religious and civil purposes. Harvard's founders, for instance, believed that there was no true knowledge or wisdom "without Christ," a predictable belief in puritan New England. Yale was founded as a reaction to the secular spirit which its founders perceived in Harvard. Even though the church had no official governing role in the University of Pennsylvania or the University of Virginia, the religious spirit of the colonists pervaded these institutions along with the others.

After the colonial period came the great frontier era in America. Ethnic groups joined by new waves of immigrants poured over the Appalachian mountains and began to settle the plains of this continent. Attempting to hold fast to their religious values, treasuring their new political freedom, working hard to take advantage of their new economic opportunities, and rising to the challenge of frontier life, these groups founded colleges wherever they settled. Hundreds of colleges sprang up across America as a result of the westward movement in nineteenth-century America.

Like the colonists, the frontier people founded these colleges for the purpose of developing leadership for their churches and communities. If they were not founded by a particular church or denomination, these colleges were founded by groups of persons who had a religious purpose for their particular college. The churches had a clear vision for their adherents and the general populace of their communities: they wanted an educated clergy; they wanted spiritual growth for their members; they wanted high moral standards to prevail in their communities; they wanted the literary and civil benefits of a college education for their youth and communities; and they wanted the economic opportunities which they believed would follow a good education. The colleges were seen as integral to the spiritual, moral, cultural, and economic vision which these frontier folk had for themselves in this vast land of opportunity. They had a holistic view of life, and a religiously oriented education was essential to the pursuit of their vision. The colonial colleges provided the first form of higher education in America, and frontier colleges built upon that model.

43

What the colonial colleges and frontier colleges—from now on we will refer to them as church-related colleges—had in common were these factors: they were private rather than government-supported; they were liberal arts colleges; they were usually affiliated with a denomination and therefore they attempted to develop the spiritual and moral dimensions of their students along with the intellectual and cultural dimensions.

In the nineteenth century, as industrialization took hold in American society, the federal government attempted to assist and enrich this process through higher education. In 1862 Congress passed the Morrill Act, which established the land-grant colleges. Several important facts stand out as part of this new development.

These universities owed their existence not to the church but to the government—federal and state—which established them and funded them through tax dollars. This change—ownership, governance, and financial support by the government—marked the beginning of a profound change in the picture of higher education in America. A dual system of higher education began in this country and has prevailed since that time. Because of the doctrine of the separation of church and state, the land-grant colleges and universities could not have the same religious nature as the church-related colleges. While the land-grant colleges and universities might contain whatever religious spirit pervaded the American public, they could not officially have any tie to the church, nor could they promulgate any particular religious point of view. The ground was thus laid for a secular approach to higher education to develop alongside the religious approach already existent in America.

The curricula of the land-grant colleges and universities also differed from those of the church-related colleges. While the curricula of the church-related colleges were basically the liberal arts, the curricula of the land-grant colleges and universities focused on the applied arts and sciences, largely related to industry and agriculture. In addition, the church-related colleges were patterned after the British colleges and universities which focused on the development of the whole person, while the land-grant colleges and universities were patterned after the German universities, with their emphasis on research and their separation of the academic disciplines into specialized areas of study.

To summarize, it was primarily the church which established the colonial colleges. In part because of this sponsorship and in part because of the religious atmosphere present in the colonies, a religious spirit pervaded the colonial colleges. Similarly, because they were founded and maintained by particular denominations, the church-related colleges which sprang up along the frontier were permeated by a religious spirit. In contrast to these church-related colleges, the land-grant colleges and universities, which were founded and supported by the government, could not promulgate a religious point of view. Besides, they operated on a paradigm which focused narrowly on the intellectual development of students, rather than on the development of the whole person. Thus America came to have two different approaches to higher education.

With World War II came a change which would ultimately transform the nature of the land-grant colleges and universities. Prior to World War II, the federal government maintained its own laboratories for research. Whatever research was not carried out in government-owned laboratories was largely a private undertaking. World War II changed this pattern. During World War II, the federal government saw the advantage of wedding its research interests and activities to the universities which had spread across the country as a result of the Morrill Act. Thus research, which was becoming an increasingly important activity in our scientific and technologically oriented society, became a priority and activity of the publicly supported universities. And much of that research was supported by the federal government. This created an even closer relationship between the government—federal and state—and the public universities. Thus, this approach to higher education, which stood in contrast to that of the church-related college, grew in strength, importance, and prestige.

At the end of World War II, approximately half of America's college students were being educated in the public universities and half in the church-related colleges. The two models or approaches within the dual system of higher education were still approximately equal in significance and influence in American society at the end of World War II. Events in the decades after World War II changed all of that.

Now let us turn our attention to the changes which took place in higher education after World War II.

The Rapid Growth and Popularity of Higher Education

The post–World War II years were years of enormous growth in student population in our colleges and universities. Congress passed the Servicemen's Readjustment Act (commonly called the GI Bill) in 1944. This initiated the first spurt in what would eventually be phenomenal growth in the numbers of people in America who would attend college. The GIs who entered college after World War II set the pattern in seeking an opportunity to improve their lives to something better than their parents had.

If the GIs had an impact upon the population of America's colleges and universities, they had an even more profound impact on the notion of who went to college in America. Up until this time, college was thought to be only for the elite. Indeed, when some of the most prominent figures in higher education—including James Conant, the president of Harvard, and Robert M. Hutchins, the president of the University of Chicago—heard that the halls of higher education were to be flooded with American servicemen, they were astounded.[1] The average American had not been thought capable of handling or benefiting from a college education.

The GIs brought still another change to higher education. In some ways the education provided by the GI Bill was seen as a reward for—if not the right of—those who had served their country in the armed forces. Perhaps imperceptibly at the time,

1. Thomas N. Bonner, "The Unintended Revolution in America's Colleges Since 1940," *Change* (Sept./Oct. 1986): 44.

this caused an important shift in the minds of the American people: higher education was no longer seen as a privilege, but as a right. Closely related to this was still another change. Earlier in American history, those who went to college automatically bore a responsibility to provide leadership within their society. But the veterans had already discharged an enormous responsibility. They now cared about how a college education would help them as individuals to advance in society. That notion would pass on to students in the future, regardless of whether or not they had served their country in the armed forces.

One of the most influential events in American higher education after World War II was the launching of Sputnik by the Soviets. In 1957 the Soviet Union launched the first satellite into space. This event shocked America, its implications rippling through the American consciousness. Immediately the U.S. set out to catch up with and surpass the Soviet Union in space. The result was a new emphasis upon mathematics and the natural sciences. Parenthetically, it should be noted that this also signaled the decline of the arts and humanities. After a round of harsh criticism of the schools and colleges in America, government leaders and the general public set out to meet this new challenge.

In 1958 Congress passed the National Defense Act, which brought government—federal and state—more deeply into the business of higher education. Money poured into higher education, particularly into the natural sciences. Science facilities were built across the land and the math and natural sciences curricula flourished. Cooperation between the federal and state governments and the research universities grew to a new intensity. All of this boosted the size and prestige of the large research universities in this country, at the same time diminishing the importance and influence of the traditional liberal arts colleges. The federal government was drawn into deeper involvement in higher education.

In the years immediately following the Second World War another event was in the making, and it burst upon the American campus in the 1960s—namely, the "baby boom." This was an additional contribution, in a manner of speaking, of the GIs. Because student population had declined in the nation's colleges and universities immediately after the wave of GIs had completed their education, educators didn't see the boom coming. Thus higher education was ill prepared for what happened, making the impact of the baby boom in the 1960s all the greater.

Since the GIs felt that they had benefited from higher education, they were intent upon acquiring those benefits for their children. Thus, the college population explosion of the 1960s signaled not only the enormous growth in size of colleges and universities, but also the increasing importance which Americans gave to a college education. The notion of the importance of a college education cannot be overstated. When higher education reached its peak in the minds of Americans in the early 1960s, it would not be wrong to talk about the concept of "education as salvation." Education took on a messianic flavor in American society. To be a professor was a mark of distinction. Faculty salaries went up. Equipment poured in. Graduate schools bulged. No one questioned this new sacred realm of higher education.

Americans believed in education to an incredible extent. Thomas N. Bonner describes this "golden age of higher education": "Never again would the colleges experience the same euphoric sense that everything was now possible, that the revolution of hope and expectations was endless. Between 1960 and 1970, 5 million new students crowded onto campuses; 500 new campuses were built; faculty salaries nearly doubled. . . . [and] research opportunities dwarfed any that had ever been known; states increased their appropriations for higher education from $1.37 billion to $5.79 billion; and by decade's end the federal government accounted for $4 billion or 16 percent of all monies spent by colleges and universities."[2]

The empire of higher education in America was further built by legislation passed by Congress during the Johnson presidency, as part of the "Great Society." In 1965 Congress passed the Higher Education Act, which provided government grants to undergraduate students. With this move, the federal government be-

2. *Ibid.*, pp. 48-49.

came directly involved in helping individual students attend college. Now the federal government had jumped into the business of higher education with both feet. Not only was it providing money for research, constructing buildings, and developing curricula, but it was also helping to pay the college expenses of individual students. This development was not lost on the American public. Students and their families easily shifted from seeing education as a privilege involving sacrifice and responsibility to viewing it as a right, which the government ought to help them secure.

Then in 1972, Congress passed legislation that created the Basic Educational Opportunity Grant. This legislation provided "equal access" to higher education for the financially needy student. David Riesman writes: "Spiritual heir to the G.I. Bill, it was the most important piece of legislation since Lincoln's day, when the Morrill Act established the land-grant college system. Basic grants (along with money from related programs) now provided some $5 billion annually to 3 million American students."[3] But Riesman also reveals that the results of this legislation have not all been good: "The recent American pursuit of equal opportunity has led us to extend some sort of college education to virtually any taker, regardless of ability, willingness to pay, or quality of previous academic work."[4]

CHANGES WHICH GROWTH BROUGHT TO HIGHER EDUCATION

Just as the public universities were growing and expanding, growth was also occurring in the church-related colleges. It was not uncommon for a college to triple in size, as my alma mater did. It is important to note, however, that the growth of private-sector schools did not equal that of public-sector schools. Far from it. After the Second World War, there was a steady increase

3. David Riesman, "Beyond the '60s," *The Wilson Quarterly* (Autumn 1978): 60.
4. *Ibid.*

in the proportion of students going to public institutions. As we noted earlier, about fifty percent of America's college youth were enrolled in each sector at the end of World War II. Currently, eighty percent of American students are in the public sector while only twenty percent are in the private sector. This drastic change has meant that the public universities have come to dwarf the church-related colleges in both size and influence.

The mainline Protestant denominations faced a challenge because of this phenomenal growth in the public universities and the lower percentage of students in the church-related colleges: how to minister to college youth when by far the majority of these young people now attended the public universities. Because of their historic belief in the importance of church involvement in higher education, they accepted this challenge and attempted to adjust their ministry to this new, dynamic, and influential situation. The Protestant denominations responded through what came to be called "campus ministry." At first each denomination worked independently , but soon the mainline Protestant denominations formed cooperative campus ministries—in part because of the ecumenical movement. Located alongside of the huge universities, these campus ministries attempted to minister to the students, faculty members, and administrators of the universities. A sad, though understandable, by-product of this focus on campus ministry was that the mainline Protestant denominations lost interest in and grew less supportive of their own colleges.

Parenthetically, but not unimportantly, most of the clergy of the mainline Protestant denominations received their undergraduate training at these public universities rather than at the church-related colleges which previously had produced the clergy. Like the pharaoh in Exodus who "knew not Joseph" (Exod. 1:8), clergy rose into positions of leadership in these mainline Protestant denominations who did not know the church-related colleges.

In keeping with the tenor of the times, the public universities moved from the traditional rural location of church-related colleges to urban settings. No longer were colleges and universities to be "ivory towers" isolated from the mainstream of life; they were to be located in urban settings where they could be deeply involved in society. Or to use the language of the time, campuses were not to be "cool"—that is, remote or isolated—but rather they were to be "hot"—active and involved. When higher education was tied to the nation's destiny in the minds of Americans, colleges and universities got involved not only with research, but with social action as well. Many government leaders as well as the average American citizen were caught off guard by this partnership during the turbulent years of the late 1960s and early 1970s.

If the baby boom brought new size and importance to higher education in America, it had negative effects as well. Universities grew to the size of cities, from 10,000 students in one decade to 50,000 students a decade or two later. Education in the public sector had to be done *en masse*. And with the focus on research instead of teaching at the large, research universities, education came to be impersonal and sometimes dehumanizing.

The fact that higher education was growing so rapidly also put pressure on the graduate schools of the large universities to produce enough faculty members for the burgeoning public and private sectors. In some ways this was a nice kind of burden because it brought prestige, power, wealth, and notoriety to the graduate schools, and therefore to the universities.

The large, urban, research university was based on the Cartesian-Newtonian paradigm. More will be said about this paradigm in later chapters, but for now it is enough to know that this paradigm separated academic areas one from another. Each academic discipline had its own specialized knowledge, language, and mode of operation. Faculty members focused on smaller and smaller parts of reality within the academic community and thus became specialists. This paradigm divided up life and acted as if reality were made up basically of separate, unrelated parts. This paradigm swept higher education in the post–World War II years. Because the graduate schools were supplying faculty members for the church-related colleges as well as the public universities, the church-related colleges came to live under the Cartesian-Newtonian paradigm as much as the public universities.

Another idea prevalent in the public universities, particularly the graduate schools, was that any approach to higher education that was infused with a particular value system was not an acceptable form of higher education. Or to put it another way, an idea developed in American higher education that only a "value-free" approach to higher education was legitimate. Even some of the mainline Protestant denominations adopted this point of view, resulting in a distancing of some of the churches from their colleges and vice versa. This distancing aided only the campus ministry movement. Denominational funding of church-related colleges plummeted. Many of the church-related colleges separated from the church; some maintained denominational ties. Each church-related college charted its own course and determined its own relationship—close, distant, or non-existent—with the church. This was new territory for the church-related colleges: to find their role in society greatly diminished, the public university now their role model, and their relationship with the church in question. The world had gone topsy-turvy for the church-related college, to the joy of some and the distress of others. Quite the opposite for the large research universities, which found themselves at their zenith, more popular and more influential than ever before.

One final feature of the public university which should be mentioned resulted from a combination of factors. First of all, because of the principle of the separation of church and state, the tax-supported public university could not promote any particular religious point of view. Increasingly this came to mean that no religious point of view was incorporated in the educational process. Second, increasingly the notion prevailed that only verifiable theories or subjects were legitimate subjects for study. This notion was a product of the Cartesian-Newtonian paradigm. This either eliminated the subject of religion from the public university altogether or made it merely one subject among others. In addition, American society was increasingly pluralistic. The final result was that the public universities were secular in their understanding of and approach to life. And because the universities had such a profound effect upon the church-related colleges, secularism increased throughout higher education in America.

To summarize, by the end of the 1960s, the large, urban, secular, research university had become one of the most powerful institutions in American society. While the church-related college provided the model for higher education early in America's history, now the public university became the model. Even though the private colleges and universities might continue to claim that they provide 60 percent of the leadership in American society, the fact that 80 percent of the college graduates in American society are graduates of the public universities suggests that they have the greater influence on American society. Clearly, after World War II American higher education had entered the era of the public university.

THE DOWN SIDE OF AMERICAN HIGHER EDUCATION

America's love affair with higher education was relatively short-lived, ending as student social protest began in earnest. Students on America's campuses responded to President Kennedy's challenge to ask not what your country can do for you, but what you can do for your country. They believed that they could and should bring justice to their country. Some became deeply involved in the civil rights movements of the mid-sixties, working for a more just society. Later they became equally involved in opposing the Vietnam War, a war they believed was morally wrong. Their initially peaceful protests turned violent, a drastic change from the quiet decade of the fifties.

This social protest movement reached its peak with the bombing of a university building in Madison, Wisconsin, and the shooting of students at Kent State University by members of the Ohio National Guard. Civil and social involvement subsided nearly as rapidly as it had started, but not before it had soured much of the American public on higher education. The public looked upon these college and university students as ungrateful—privileged above all other youth—yet ungrateful. America had given more to these young people than to any other generation, and look how they responded! Perhaps higher education wasn't so great after all. This reaction marked the beginning of a lengthy period of disillusionment with higher education in American society.

The 1970s were much quieter years on the nation's campuses. A number of factors contributed to the students' declining interest in their society and world and increasing focus on themselves: the loss of charismatic leaders like President John F. Kennedy, his brother Robert Kennedy, and Dr. Martin Luther King, Jr.; disillusionment with less than admirable government leaders; the continued nuclear threat; and perhaps fear of the possible consequences of further social unrest. The aftertaste of the Vietnam War lingered in American society. Watergate increased the students' disillusionment with their country and intensified their focus on themselves and their own well-being.

Tougher economic times also had an impact upon students. They became more concerned about their own future, and less concerned about the future of their country. On campus this meant a narrower focus on career preparation. The arts and humanities fell further into disrepute in this increasingly utilitarian atmosphere.

After the "tradition-bashing" of the 1960s, the curriculum on many campuses changed from a more traditional selection of courses with a firm set of requirements which all students had to fulfill, to a more innovative and expanded curriculum exploring a host of new subjects, as the colleges and universities attempted to keep up with the knowledge explosion. In addition, requirements dropped to a minimum in what some people called a "smorgasbord" approach to higher education. The 1960s saw a push for freedom—freedom from tradition and rules, and from persons in authority—freedom for the individual to do what he or she chose. It was the era of the "do-your-own-thing ethic," and the era of the sexual revolution. Self-discipline gave way to self-expression and self-fulfillment.

While the country appreciated the quieter campuses, there was a lingering scar on the nation left by the violent sixties. The country would not soon forgive its seemingly ungrateful youth. As a result of the lingering anger over the campus unrest of the sixties, and propelled by the economic woes which struck the nation in the 1970s, Americans developed a skeptical attitude toward higher education, questioning the social involvement of students in the late sixties and early seventies, and the diversity which developed out of the rapid growth of higher education and the knowledge explosion. Particularly as the recession hit in the first half of the 1970s, questions were raised as to whether all of this higher education was needed and whether it was affordable. Should all of these students be in college? Didn't society also need persons trained in the trades? Does education benefit the student alone or should the whole good of the society also be part of the equation? If so, should the state be paying for such a large proportion of each student's education? What is the relationship between the needs of society and the programs offered at the universities? Who should set policy?

With this new, highly diverse but burgeoning system of higher education, America was trying to find its way in new territory. When growth in this system peaked, few, if any, questions were asked; in the 1970s, questions were being asked to which there were few answers. By the end of the seventies, however, one fact was beginning to emerge: the percentage of the nation's financial resources going to higher education was in sharp decline.[5]

One further point must be made about the 1970s. The social reforms of the 1960s and the federal higher education legislation of the 1970s began to have an impact as larger and larger numbers of women, blacks, and poor people entered college. Bonner illustrates this change with the following statistics: "An astonishing 77 percent of the 3.5 million new students who came to college in the '70s were women. For the first time since the founding of Harvard in 1636, women outnumbered men in college. Even in graduate study, the number of women pursuing advanced degrees of all kinds equaled that of men by 1980. By the latter year, too, the enrollment of blacks, which had been climbing steadily since the mid-'60s, passed the million mark and ac-

5. Bonner, p. 50.

counted for 10 percent of all college students."[6] Thus, while there was discontinuity with the 1960s at some points, the 1970s also displayed at least one continuity: the coming to fruition of some of the goals which came out of the 1960s.

American higher education was troubled by further difficulties during the 1980s. The high inflation which plagued America during the first half of the decade had a serious impact upon higher education. Inflation caused the cost of a college education to soar, though even then the full impact of inflation was not passed on to the students. Coupled with this was a concerted effort to curtail the federal government's involvement in higher education. This only compounded the financial pinch for students and their parents.

Precisely at this time, several important studies of higher education were carried out, and the reports indicated that America's higher educational system lacked quality. The major study, carried out by the Carnegie Foundation for the Advancement of Teaching, and authored by Ernest L. Boyer, was entitled *College: The Undergraduate Experience in America.*[7] This and other similar studies seemed to confirm what the American public already felt: the rapid growth of higher education, coupled with a change in philosophy that encouraged anyone to attend college; and the large amount of money pouring into higher education, had all eroded the quality of higher education in America. The point of view which prevailed in America from the 1950s to the early 1970s and the point of view which developed in the mid-1970s and carried over into the 1980s collided. Higher education would no longer be the unquestioned institution that it had been in previous decades.

In this atmosphere, calls went out for better quality in higher education, for clearer purposes within the institutions and within the entire national enterprise of higher education; for less duplication of programs within and between institutions, for more accountability, and for more careful assessment of the "out-

---

6. *Ibid.*
7. Ernest L. Boyer, *College: The Undergraduate Experience in America* (New York: Harper & Row, 1987).

comes" of courses, programs, and institutions. The 1980s began to produce a kind of "shakedown" of all that had developed in higher education since the Second World War. America was attempting to find its way into the future of higher education, basing its direction on more clearly reasoned and more carefully considered policies. These factors only further eroded the opinion many Americans had of higher education.

Accompanying America's diminishing impression of higher education were other critical developments. A general mood of self-doubt and pessimism came out of Vietnam, Watergate, and the Iran-Contra affair. In addition, Americans were alarmed by the nation's apparent decline in the world economy. The fact that America has become a debtor nation worried many Americans, and the stock market crash of the fall of 1987 didn't improve America's self-confidence. These developments cannot be separated from the view which Americans had of higher education. In short, the messianic view which Americans had of higher education in the 1960s was gone; that view was replaced with very mixed feelings about higher education.

These mixed feelings are best observed by looking at what is happening to enrollment in higher education in the late 1980s. On the one hand, far fewer 18-year-olds are available for higher education. On the other hand, instead of declining as all of the demographers had predicted, enrollment levels are holding steady, because non-traditional students are entering college at a very rapid rate. The average age of college students has risen sharply. Forty-five percent of all college students—undergraduate and graduate—are over age 25. In spite of all of the criticism being leveled at colleges and universities, Americans are enrolling in greater numbers than ever before. Apparently they believe that they can have a better life as a result of attending college. Or to put it another way, Americans are seeing that the less education they have, the closer to the bottom of the totem pole, economically and socially, they will be for the rest of their lives. So even though Americans are criticizing higher education, they are taking advantage of it more than ever before.

Many colleges revised their curricula during the 1980s,

abandoning the "smorgasbord" and highly proliferated curricula of the 1960s and 1970s in favor of smaller and more prescribed curricula. Instead of focusing on new information, students were required to spend a considerable amount of time on a common core of information. Thus, the freedom of the 1960s and 1970s was curtailed by faculties who spent a considerable amount of time attempting to identify a common body of knowledge that all students should acquire.

The cost of higher education rose sharply during the 1980s, far more than costs of higher education, far above costs in most other areas of the economy. This rise in cost became the focus of national attention. To many Americans it seemed ironic that the cost of higher education was rising precisely when its quality was in question. But many American families were less concerned with the irony than they were with the threat that a college education would soon be out of their reach. The federal government decreased its support of higher education. The states were unable to take up the slack. Therefore a greater responsibility for the cost of education fell to families, a burden which Secretary of Education William Bennett believed to be appropriate since it was the individual student who benefited. Others did not see the issue that simply. They realized that, while the individual student is the chief beneficiary, society also benefits; society needs a highly educated population. Regardless, in the 1980s a national discussion ensued on the topic of the high cost of a college education.

Finally, a critical topic with far-reaching implications emerged during the 1980s: How will America finance its dual higher-educational enterprise in the future? Up until the 1980s, private higher education was funded by student tuition and by private gifts. In contrast, public higher education was funded with tax funds in addition to student tuition. This was the long-standing pattern of financing in our dual system of higher education, one established when the land-grant institutions joined the private colleges and universities as America's system of higher education.

This pattern began to change in the 1970s when students,

projects, and programs in private colleges began receiving federal aid. Some states also set aside funds to go to students attending private colleges. Thus, the fiscal lines began to blur. Subsequently, massive changes began to take place which have all but obliterated the traditional fiscal lines between the private and public sectors of higher education. Public universities began to carry out fund-raising efforts in the private sector to supplement the funds they received from state legislatures. For example, in past decades approximately 35 private colleges in Ohio banded together each year to raise approximately $3 million from the private sector, which they subsequently divided proportionally among themselves. In the second half of the 1980s, the Ohio State University carried out a three-year $350 million campaign *in the private sector*. So we must be prepared to see new developments in the funding relationship between the private and public sectors in American higher education.

Changes in the Church-Related College

As we have seen, since the Second World War the church-related college, once the model for higher education, was dwarfed in size and influence by the large research university. No longer the leader in modeling higher education, the church-related college lost its way in the shadow of the large, urban, secular, research university and became its mimic.

Some positive things did happen to the church-related college in the growth decades. The simple growth in individual size of these colleges gave each of them more faculty members and students, and provided them with a richer intellectual life. Second, just as the rest of higher education basked in greater affluence after World War II, so did the church-related college. Better facilities and a better paid faculty helped to boost the academic programs of these colleges. Furthermore, some kudos are due these colleges for the role they play in the education of minority students. In Ohio, for example, the private, mostly church-related colleges enroll a larger percentage of minority students than do the state-supported institutions—9.5 percent of the total student enrollment of private institutions compared with 6.5 percent of the total enrollment of the state-supported colleges and universities.[8]

However, too much of what has happened to the church-related colleges in recent decades has been negative. When in the mid- to late-1950s the mainline denominations responded to exploding college enrollment rates by developing and funding campus ministry, they took on an excessive burden. The mainline denominations felt compelled—and rightly so—to be a presence on the university campus. But with limited dollars for education—along with the rising percentage of their own students choosing the university over the church-related college—these denominations cut back funds for their own colleges, a trend that has continued to be present.

At the same time, some of these denominations began to advocate disaffiliation from their colleges. The effects of this we have already noted. Clearly, by the end of the fifties, the relationship between many church-related colleges and their denominations had loosened considerably from what it had been before the war. Consequently, the nature and mission of these colleges also changed.

The rapid growth of the church-related colleges in the 1960s—some of them doubled or tripled in size in a decade—made them vulnerable. In most of these colleges staff and students could no longer fit into the chapel at one time and thereby the colleges lost one of the most important means of interpreting their unique ethos, identity, and their mission to their students. Second, the 1960s brought a general assault on tradition within American society, and it was felt on these campuses. Many traditions which had helped to transmit the values and ethos of these colleges were overturned; at a time when other factors were also creating change.

The influx of students on these campuses did not follow old

8. "Minding the Future" (1986-87 case support statement of the Ohio Foundation of Independent Colleges).

patterns; and the homogeneity of many of these colleges was lost. The heterogeneity, welcomed though it was, came when the colleges were vulnerable. Thus the changed student body in turn brought changes to these colleges.

Faculty additions brought change too. Obviously, growth in the student body meant growth in the size of the faculty. As the student population in higher education grew, there was a great need for professors. The church-related colleges, experiencing this same need, turned to the young graduates just coming out of the graduate schools of the large research universities. Thus, into these changing, vulnerable colleges came bright, young faculty members who brought with them the viewpoint and values of the large, urban, secular, research university. Some church-related colleges may have welcomed this viewpoint; others had no choice. Despite their humaneness and smaller size, the church-related colleges borrowed many university ways, including the "smorgasbord" approach to curriculum which pervaded higher education in the 1960s and 1970s. In addition, the question of quality which has been raised during the eighties is just as applicable to the church-related college as it is to the public university.

So the question which has arisen in the minds of many persons has to do with the mission and purpose of the church-related college at the end of the 1980s. What is the *raison d'être* of the church-related college? Is there anything more than a difference in size between it and the public university? What is distinctive about the church-related college?

4. A Critical Analysis of the Public University, the Church-Related College, and the Church

THE PUBLIC UNIVERSITY

Since the Second World War, if not before, the public university has been operating according to an outdated, harmful paradigm.

Most of us live comfortably with the notion that the world is just as we perceive it. For centuries, scientists led us to believe that if they pursued their "value-free" hypotheses according to the scientific method, they would arrive at the truth. Now, however, scientists believe that what they see and the results of the experiments they carry out depend upon the paradigm in which they are operating; that the paradigm provides the glasses through which they view reality and it affects what they see and what they do. In addition, many scientists are now saying that the paradigm under which they have been operating and through which they have been perceiving reality is inaccurate. They believe that we must exchange that old paradigm by which we have been living for several centuries for another one, and we must be prepared for some radical changes in our thinking.

The person most closely associated with the word *paradigm* is Thomas S. Kuhn, author of *The Structure of Scientific Revolutions*.[1] While Kuhn devotes the better part of this volume to dis-

---

1. Thomas S. Kuhn, *The Structure of Scientific Revolutions* (Chicago: University of Chicago Press, 1962).

cussing the concept of paradigm, he fails to give an explicit definition of the word. Therefore, while I am using his thoughts, I will have to attempt to describe the concept myself.

Kuhn uses the term *paradigm* in describing the work of scientists. According to Kuhn, scientists do not approach their subject with a clean slate, as was previously believed, but with a particular set of shared assumptions and biases. This shared mind-set or viewpoint is a paradigm. As Ian Barbour explains:

> There are no *bare uninterpreted* data. Expectations and conceptual commitments influence perceptions, both in everyday life and in science. Man supplies the categories of interpretation, right from the start. The very language in which observations are reported is influenced by prior theories. The predicates we use in describing the world and the categories with which we classify events depend on the kinds of regularities we anticipate. The presuppositions which the scientist brings to his enquiry are reflected in the way he formulates a problem, the kind of apparatus he builds, and the type of variable he considers important.[2]

Coming at this topic in a slightly different fashion, Barbour points out that:

> In becoming a member of a particular scientific or religious community, a person acknowledges its exemplars and comes to adopt its assumptions and expectations. Neither science nor religion is an individual enterprise; a person interprets his experience within a communal tradition. The concept of paradigm keeps before us the importance of a community of shared purposes, attitudes and presuppositions.[3]

Scientists form a model out of their shared mind-set or set of assumptions. They follow a common pattern *as if it were true.* Just as an accepted judicial pattern provides judges with a working point of view, so a paradigm provides scientists with a working point of view. The paradigm of a given group of scientists guides

---

2. Ian G. Barbour, *Myths, Models, and Paradigms: A Comparative Study in Science and Religion* (New York: Harper & Row, 1974), p. 95.
3. *Ibid.,* p. 147.

their research. It suggests what questions may legitimately be asked, what techniques may be fruitful, and what types of solutions are admissible. Again Barbour is helpful:

> Most scientific endeavor is carried on within the framework of such a "received tradition" which defines the kinds of explanation to be sought. . . . The tradition influences the concepts through which the scientist sees the world, the expectations by which his work is governed, and the language he uses.[4]

Kuhn and other proponents of this view of paradigm are asking us to make a one hundred eighty degree turn in our understanding of how scientists work. Instead of being value-free, instead of letting the evidence lead where it will, scientists actually work within a paradigm which influences what they see, accept, and report. The paradigm controls the scientists. Harold K. Schilling points out that

> knowledge is both a product of perception and a frame of reference or a probe which makes perception and conception possible. In other words, what we *do see* is determined to a considerable extent by what we *have seen and conceived* and by what we suppose or believe *can be seen*. It is amazing how difficult it is at times to see—say, through a microscope—what one does not expect to see, and how easy it is to see what one does expect, even though it may not be there to be seen. This is the case in complex experimentation and long-range research as well as in simple observation; in corporate as well as individual experience.[5]

Ian Barbour writes: "Like solving a puzzle or playing a game of chess, normal science seeks solutions within an accepted framework; the rules of the game are already established. . . . Paradigms determine the way a scientist sees the world."[6]

Once a paradigm is established, the work of most scientists

4. Ian G. Barbour, *Issues in Science and Religion* (Englewood Cliffs, NJ: Prentice-Hall, 1966), p. 154.
5. Harold K. Schilling, *The New Consciousness in Science and Religion* (Philadelphia: United Church Press, 1973), p. 52.
6. Barbour, *Myths*, pp. 104-5.

is, as Kuhn puts it, "mopping up," fitting into the paradigm—even forcing into the paradigm—as much of nature as possible.

> Closely examined, whether historically or in the contemporary laboratory, that enterprise seems an attempt to force nature into the preformed and relatively inflexible box that the paradigm supplies. No part of the aim of normal science is to call forth new sets of phenomena; indeed those that will not fit into the box are often not seen at all.[7]

The tendency, therefore, is for a given paradigm to prevail for a long period of time—for centuries, or even millennia.

To be accepted as a paradigm, one theory must seem better than another. Yet no paradigm explains all phenomena. Kuhn points out that "the emergence of new theories is generally preceded by a period of pronounced professional insecurity. As one might expect, that insecurity is generated by the persistent failure of the puzzles of normal science to come out as they should. Failure of existing rules is the prelude to a search for new ones."[8]

Paradigms are mutually exclusive. As Barbour puts it, "a new paradigm requires the overthrow of the old, not just an addition to previous theories."[9] As anomalies grow in number, the pressure builds and a sense of crisis leads the scientific community to search for alternative theories. A new paradigm may then be proposed, one which challenges the old paradigm and promises to answer the dilemmas it posed. Thus the new paradigm *replaces* the old.

The far-reaching effects of a new paradigm lead to a revolution.[10] Kuhn points out that "when the transition [from the old to the new paradigm] is complete, the profession will have changed its view of the field, its methods, and its goals."[11] Furthermore, "when paradigms change, the world itself changes with them. Led by a new paradigm, scientists adopt new instruments and look in new places. Even more important, during rev-

---

7. Kuhn, p. 24.
8. *Ibid.,* p. 68.
9. Barbour, *Issues,* p. 154.
10. Barbour, *Myths,* p. 104.
11. Kuhn, p. 85.

olutions scientists see new and different things when looking with familiar instruments in places they have looked before."[12] A change in paradigm opens up new insights, releases new energy, and reveals new relationships.

It is important for the reader to understand that what Kuhn says about scientists is true of us as well. We all work from a common paradigm. It is only a matter of time after scientists have established a new paradigm that the general public also bases its estimate of reality on the new paradigm. For example, it was only a matter of time after Copernicus established a new paradigm about the arrangement of the planets, one which rejected the paradigm established by Ptolemy, that this view of reality prevailed among the general public. Thus, the concept of a paradigm is not reserved for scientists, nor is its importance felt only by the scientific community. It becomes the prevailing way in which society perceives life, and changing from one paradigm to another is often a painful and protracted process for any society.

We are living in a time when scientists are changing the paradigm by which they approach reality and thus are shaping a new consciousness. Harold Schilling writes:

> This is precisely what many observers see actually transpiring today on a grand scale. And they see it to be attributable in large measure to the impact upon man of contemporary twentieth-century science—now called *post modern science*—to distinguish it from *modern science,* its predecessor of the seventeenth, eighteenth and nineteenth centuries, which was in many respects very different.[13]

The paradigm which shaped human consciousness since Descartes, Newton, and Bacon can no longer handle the new views of persons like Darwin, Einstein, Heisenberg, Bohr, and Gödel. As a result, a new paradigm has been established in science, and the usual effects of the establishment of a new paradigm are currently taking place. Schilling describes these changes:

12. *Ibid.,* p. 110.
13. Schilling, pp. 17-18.

> The human imagination is being amplified. Men's minds and hearts are being liberated from inhibiting attitudes and conceptions to which they had fallen prey in the modern era, so they are now able to explore realms and dimensions of reality from which they had been blocked until recently.[14]

New insights are available, new energy is being unleashed, and new relationships are being observed. It is indeed an exciting, creative, and opportune time.

Having established the concept of paradigm and having suggested that we live in a time when a general change in paradigm is just beginning, we need to focus next on the concept of paradigm and its effects on human consciousness as these relate to American higher education.

The paradigm which scientists have been abandoning in the twentieth century is sometimes referred to as the paradigm of "modern science," and the new paradigm which is in the process of being adopted by scientists is sometimes called the "post-modern" paradigm. For the purposes of this book, I will refer to the paradigm of modern science as the "Cartesian-Newtonian" paradigm and to the new paradigm of integration and wholeness as the "post-modern science" paradigm.

A more detailed description is needed of the paradigm of modern science—the Cartesian-Newtonian paradigm—and its impact upon higher education, along with the reasons why it has been rejected by scientists.

Harold K. Schilling points out that according to the Cartesian-Newtonian paradigm, "the world was closed, essentially completed and unchanging, basically substantive, simple and shallow, and fundamentally unmysterious—a rigidly programmed machine. . . . Moreover, it was thought that since nature was without doubt rigidly deterministic there *could* be no radically new developments or genuine surprises."[15] According to the Cartesian-Newtonian paradigm, the universe was comparable to a machine; by contrast, the new paradigm uses an or-

14. *Ibid.*, p. 18.
15. *Ibid.*, pp. 44-45.

ganism as its model. While Descartes and others believed in God, they saw God as the creator of this vast world-machine who then abandoned it to run its course. Scientists felt that this paradigm had a finality about it, that all of the fundamental principles of the physical world were known.

Referring to the Cartesian-Newtonian paradigm, the 1898-1899 catalog of the University of Chicago stated that "it seems probable that most of the grand underlying principles have been firmly established and that further advances are to be sought chiefly in the vigorous application of these principles to all the phenomena which come under our notice."[16] The author of this catalog was not aware that at the very same time, scientists in various parts of the world—largely physicists and mathematicians—were experiencing the frustrations of a paradigm which simply would not handle their new observations and equations. They were glimpsing the outlines of a radically new paradigm.

Within the Cartesian-Newtonian paradigm, reality, like a machine, was made up of many parts. Each of these parts was an entity unto itself which could be isolated, observed, understood, and then controlled. Isaac Newton perfected the mechanistic nature of this paradigm. Douglas Bowman points out that, under Newton, this paradigm split reality into ever more simple, static, and supposedly independent entities. The sense of the dynamic, living, organismic, and often mysterious connectedness of reality was lost.[17] Descartes held to a mind-body dualism which sacrificed man's organismic nature. Like a machine, and like the physical world, the human was understood through its broken-down parts.

One of the most critical aspects of the Cartesian-Newtonian paradigm to understand is that it changed from being a paradigm which explained only the physical world to a paradigm which explained the *metaphysical* world as well. As Ian Barbour describes it: "The concepts of Newtonian physics, which had been so su-

16. *Ibid.*, p. 45.
17. Douglas C. Bowman, "Toward a Post-Modern Ethic," *Pacific Theological Review* (Spring 1987): 41.

perbly successful in astronomy and mechanics, were increasingly adopted as an all-encompassing metaphysical scheme. . . . A technique of investigation was on its way to becoming a total account of the world; a *method* was being turned into a *metaphysics*."[18]

Earlier I described how reality might be forced into a paradigm. This is what began to happen. Only that which could be handled by the scientific method—the methodology of the Cartesian-Newtonian paradigm—was real and valid. Thus, while the Cartesian-Newtonian paradigm was meant to pursue a description of nature—that is, *how nature worked*—many scientists as well as the general public operated as if *all questions* within the universe could be handled within this paradigm by its indigenous methodology. Thus, anything beyond the physical had to be validated by the scientific method, or it would often be denied.

I have gone to considerable length to describe the nature and role of a paradigm because the Cartesian-Newtonian paradigm has shaped the public university, and the public university has been the model for all of higher education in America since World War II. Indeed, it has shaped much of American society as well. Several features of the impact of the Cartesian-Newtonian paradigm upon the public university are important to understand.

The first is that the Cartesian-Newtonian paradigm breaks all knowledge down into its smallest parts and in the process isolates one part of knowledge from another. The two critical concepts here are *separation* and *isolation*. As a result of the dominance of this paradigm over the life of the public university, all knowledge is divided into separate academic disciplines. Each academic area has its own specialized body of knowledge, its own procedures, and its own language. Faculty members—who are often researchers as well—focus on smaller and smaller parts, becoming specialists in their own narrow fields.

This paradigm chops up life, so that reality seems to be made up of separate, unrelated parts instead of being a system. The curricula of the public universities are organized around this Car-

18. Barbour, *Issues*, p. 36.

tesian-Newtonian paradigm. Universities pursue learning in departments, divisions, colleges, and graduate schools, all of which are separated from one another on the basis of the Cartesian-Newtonian paradigm. One wag has said that the only unifying factor in the contemporary American university is the faculty's common concern over parking. Students are left to themselves to put knowledge back together again—if they ever can.

It is not hard to see how pervasively American society is influenced by this paradigm and approach to higher education. Individualism has flourished in American society while human connectedness and interdependence have waned. Management techniques have been drawn from this paradigm, making humans feel manipulated and used, like parts of a machine. The assembly line would not have been invented without this paradigm. This paradigm also created the expert or specialist whose word cannot be questioned. And ethical behavior has suffered because we tend to focus on one small part of an enterprise without feeling any responsibility for the whole of the enterprise.

American higher education has been populated with specialists. A faculty member basically stays within a given academic department, perhaps even within some smaller section of that department. Separation and isolation have shaped the educational process to which students are exposed. Milton Reigelman calls to mind an historic address which Ralph Waldo Emerson delivered before the Harvard faculty in which he pointed out that their understanding of what it means to be a scholar was so limited it was crippling. Said Emerson: "The state of society is one in which members have suffered amputation from the trunk, and walk about as so many walking monsters—a good finger, a good neck, a stomach, an elbow, but never a man." Reigelman points out that what Emerson railed against in 1837 is still happening 150 years later:

> The required credential for admission to academe today is the doctoral dissertation, typically written during a year or more of reclusion, on a restricted and narrow topic and in a style tailored to one or two specialists on a committee. . . . Our system, from start to fin-

ish, is set up to produce specialists, not scholars. As undergraduates, we select isolated courses and major in discrete disciplines. Beyond the college level, we are trained to be specialists, we write our articles for and deliver our papers to specialists, and we design and teach our courses as specialists. We think of ourselves not as scholars, but as biologists or art historians or mathematicians—"a good finger, a good neck, a stomach, an elbow, but never a man."[19]

Missing from higher education is the sense of connectedness. Ernest Boyer comments that on too many campuses "students wander from one narrow department requirement to another never discovering connections, never seeking the whole."[20]

Specialists perpetuate the mechanistic treatment of humans as parts, rather than as whole beings. David Brown tells this story:

I remember sitting at large conference tables watching professionals put the finishing touches on a big corporate deal or a multi-million dollar public project—each of them performing a very specific task, but never asked and never expecting to participate beyond the narrow boundaries of their acknowledged competence. I saw an analyst using her calculator to number crunch a set of anticipated interest rates; a lawyer whispering to his client about a forthcoming IRS opinion needed to close the deal; a planner fidgeting with color slides showing the technical stages of a proposed construction schedule— men and women whom no one in the room really knew.[21]

Only one part of a person—a specific skill, for example—is of value, not the whole person; only that which qualifies a person as a specialist is of value. By isolating specialists from the total project, we seemingly take away their ethical responsibility for the whole project. Recently Kurt Waldheim indicated that he did not know the meaning of the total project of the Nazis in which he played only a part. Earlier Adolf Eichmann pleaded innocent

19. Milton Reigelman, "Today's Scholar," *The Chronicle of Higher Education,* 2 September 1987, p. A128.

20. Boyer, *College,* p. 90.

21. David W. Brown, "Professional Virtue: A Dangerous Kind of Humbug" *Change* (November/December 1985): 46.

of participating in the Holocaust because, as he said, "I was only in transportation." *Ludicrous* is an inadequate description of such mental and spiritual gymnastics carried out under the logic of specialization in accordance with the Cartesian-Newtonian paradigm.

Specialization by definition separates one practitioner from another. The Cartesian-Newtonian paradigm puts distance between people because it has first made specialists out of them. Their competence makes them disconnected rather than connected. It isolates them from one another instead of uniting them.

Still another unfortunate consequence of specialization is the impact it has on personal and social ethics and therefore upon society as a whole. David Brown points out that competence is not a virtue in itself. Professional competence is only of instrumental value. "If you make competence a virtue, an end in itself, you have no grounds for finally determining the value of what you know or do or for evaluating what others know or do."[22] By making people into competent professionals and by making competence a virtue, we automatically make whatever these persons do as professionals virtuous or ethical. "Creating tax shelters for the rich becomes no better or worse an activity than caring for the homeless in shelters of a different kind. Programming the computer simulation of a nuclear exchange for the Joint Chiefs of Staff has the same merit as developing a medical protocol for the burn unit of a metropolitan hospital."[23] Some very unethical things have been done by specialists and professionals in this country—Watergate and the Iran-Contra episode are two good examples. The sense of personal responsibility for ourselves, others, and our whole society has been greatly diminished because of our focus on specialization and competence.

Specialization has become identified with competence. More than any other factor in academe, this specialist approach to education has led to ethical irresponsibility. Only the person

22. *Ibid.*
23. *Ibid.*

trained in biology can address biological issues; only the person trained in ethics can address ethical issues, ad infinitum. But this is precisely the thought process and pattern of behavior being conveyed in the university operating under the Cartesian-Newtonian paradigm. Hunter R. Rawlings writes:

> The purpose of a liberal education has always been to enable students to see things whole. Today, however, the academic department structure makes that goal almost impossible to achieve at most colleges and universities by compartmentalizing knowledge mercilessly. . . . At the undergraduate level, the department structure creates the following type of problem: As a freshman, a student signs up for a course in the art department, which focuses on French painters but deals little with their country or language. As a sophomore, he or she takes beginning French in the language department, and a course in the English department that includes novels by Balzac, Flaubert, and Stendhal. As a junior, the student signs up for a course on the French Revolution in the history department and, as a senior, studies structuralism in the anthropology department.
>
> By the time that student graduates, he has had a series of courses from which he has probably learned a great deal—but he has not once in four years been encouraged to see that the courses are in any way connected. In fact, the essential relationship among them has been effectively obscured, because what he learned in one was separated and sealed off from what he learned in the others.[24]

A college president, Howard Lowry wrote at mid-century: "American academic life is full of men and women who are quite content to stay within the enchantment of their own activity. They have no impulse for pursuing larger meanings, or often even the meaning of their own speciality."[25] The result is not so much education as it is job training, not so much the pursuit of life's ultimate questions as it is indoctrination into disciplines, not so much awe and mystery as job-training, not so much a de-

24. Hunter R. Rawlings III, "The Basic Mission of Higher Education Is Thwarted by Academic Departments," *The Chronicle of Higher Education,* 14 Oct. 1987, p. B2.

25. Howard Lowry, *The Mind's Adventure: Religion and Higher Education* (Philadelphia: Westminster Press, 1950), p. 77.

scription of connectedness and relationships as the pursuit of parts. Students are treated as less than the whole persons they are and wish to be.

The second important feature of the Cartesian-Newtonian paradigm that has shaped the public university is that it held to a closed view of the universe. This paradigm holds that all information is available and knowable because the universe is a closed entity. In addition, many scientists—as well as philosophers— have held to a reductionist view that reality can be known only through empirical observation. If something cannot be observed and verified, it does not exist. Transcendence is thus excluded; all mystery and awe are ruled out of life.

The Cartesian-Newtonian paradigm had such a strong hold on scientific thinking during the past several centuries that even Einstein took little note of those experimental discoveries that have since undermined this paradigm and suggested a new one.[26] Under the heavy weight of the Cartesian-Newtonian paradigm, the cosmos seemed empty of surprises. However, recently it has come to light that Newton entertained "fanciful" ideas that the universe might not be as mechanistic, as closed, as complete, or as predictable as he and others thought. Newton kept such thoughts to himself; manuscripts which made such suggestions he locked up in a black box. Newton was guilty of suppressing mystery and hope in order to keep a tidy paradigm.[27]

Having this view of the universe has affected the public university in several ways. First and foremost, it has ruled out transcendence. If only verifiable data is acceptable, then the concept of God is ruled out. Because the Cartesian-Newtonian paradigm focused only on the physical realm and because only that for which there was empirical evidence was real, theology went from being central to being peripheral. God became a problem and theology had to work in an increasingly hostile environment.

It has been difficult for the Christian faith to function, let

26. Freeman J. Dyson, *Infinite in All Directions: An Exploration of Science and Belief* (New York: Harper & Row, 1988), p. 45.

27. *Ibid.*, p. 50.

alone flourish, in this atmosphere. The spiritual dimension of humans is deemphasized, if not denied. Theologians in this climate have been hard pressed to relate God to the universe. In hindsight, with eyes that are not limited by the Cartesian-Newtonian paradigm, we can see why faith has languished in academe.

Not only did the Cartesian-Newtonian paradigm negate the spiritual dimension, but according to it the universe was complete, understandable, and therefore controllable. Not only did spirituality atrophy; the universe lost its mystery and we lost our sense of awe. Many people in the Western world, where the Cartesian-Newtonian paradigm has been dominant, are spiritual dwarfs. Even those who practice faith and piety are relatively shallow when it comes to spirituality. It is not a coincidence that in the 1960s and 1970s many young people who rejected much of American society turned to Eastern religions which call for and exercise a great deal of the spiritual capacity of the human.

In addition to the loss of transcendence and mystery, two additional factors made faith difficult in the public university. America became a more pluralistic society after World War II. The Waspish point of view which had prevailed in America diminished in influence amid the growth and influence of other groups. It became more difficult to operate in America as if the old monolithic system was still intact.

Coupled with this pluralism was the religious neutrality of the university, a condition due to its government sponsorship. Add to this the fact that secularism was increasingly influential in American society and it is not hard to see that the public university—wittingly or unwittingly—became the proponent of a secular interpretation of life.

Let me mention one other critical factor in this picture. The opinion arose in the public university that all teaching should be "value-free," a product of the scientific method. Any faculty member worth his or her salt was to be objective not only in carrying out research but also in teaching. They were not to take a values point of view; they were not to intrude into that dimension of the students' lives. This value-free approach to higher education created a vacuum in higher education which secularism filled with little effort.

The graduate schools produced new faculty members who were initiates into the Cartesian-Newtonian paradigm, who were locked into the particular body of knowledge, methodology, tools, and jargon of their particular academic discipline. The Cartesian-Newtonian paradigm thus took a stranglehold on the universities.

One final remark about the public universities should be made. After World War II, public universities grew to such size that the educational enterprise there—particularly at the undergraduate level—can only be termed "mass education." There is something ironic about the phrase "mass education." Can education really be done *en masse*? Are not humans so different, so unique, that education must be a personal activity? The large numbers of students filling university lecture halls encourage an approach to undergraduate education that dehumanizes and bureaucratizes the educational process. What we have gained in the number of persons in our society earning an undergraduate degree we may well be losing in the nature and quality of that educational process.

THE CHURCH-RELATED COLLEGE

As we have already noted, the public university grew in influence as well as in size following the Second World War. As the church-related college was increasingly influenced and then dominated by the public university, it also came to be dominated by the Cartesian-Newtonian paradigm. The population explosion in both the public and private sectors of higher education during the 1960s caused a shortage of teachers. Hard pressed to meet this need for additional faculty members, the church-related colleges looked to the burgeoning graduate schools of the public universities. These new, young faculty members recruited by the church-related colleges had received their training under the Cartesian-Newtonian paradigm. Like their teachers and mentors at the public universities, they divided knowledge into small areas and became specialists in their own areas. Many were trained in research and had earned their degree by producing a dissertation on some minute part of their academic field. The result was that the Cartesian-Newtonian paradigm came to dominate the thinking of the church-related college as much as the public university.

The church-related colleges began to organize their curricula according to the Cartesian-Newtonian paradigm, into separate academic disciplines, and specialized academic departments. Perhaps even more detrimental was the fact that the new faculty members trained in the public universities carried with them the belief that a truly excellent education was a value-free education, that faculty members should take a value-free stance in the classroom. The result was that the academic programs of these church-related colleges no longer helped to build and sustain the unique point of view of the college. It was the time of the "do-your-own-thing ethic" in America. The values vacuum in the church-related college was quickly filled with the secular air which American higher education was breathing.

While the church-related colleges had once relied upon each individual faculty member to share his or her values with students, in this new atmosphere this became less likely. Whereas once faculty members attempted to describe their faith to students or attempted to stimulate faith in chapel presentations, this now became less likely. The colleges hired chaplains—themselves specialists under the Cartesian-Newtonian paradigm—to carry out a program of ministry on the church-related college campus. But under the Cartesian-Newtonian paradigm which denied transcendence, the lone attempts of these chaplains and ministries to demonstrate and instill faith through an effort which was now peripheral were in stark contrast to the days when faith was central to the nature and mission of the college and when all faculty members shared, nurtured, and propagated each college's unique ethos. In addition, because of the growth and new diversity of the student population in the church-related college, chapel programs were no longer an effective means of shaping and transmitting values. Faith became a mere addendum at many church-related colleges—though this was not always deliberate. Faith lost its unifying and energizing role and had to take a backseat to the various academic areas.

The inroads the value-free point of view had made into both the church and affiliated colleges contributed to weakening ties between the two. Some sponsoring denominations wanted ties cut with their colleges. Some of the colleges agreed, either cutting ties with their denominations or maintaining "historic" ties with their denominations or maintaining "historic" ties at a distance.

As a result, both parties were losers. The colleges lost their ties with the church. The church lost a resource—for many church-related colleges, the training of clergy was lost to the university.

Not only were the academic programs of the church-related colleges affected by the Cartesian-Newtonian paradigm; so was college organization. The college administrative structure was divided into separate areas according to specialities. Student life, financial aid, admissions, counseling, maintenance, housing, and ministry were some of the specialized administrative departments which became common at the church-related college. Management techniques which were the products of the Cartesian-Newtonian paradigm were also introduced. As a result the entire college administrative structure was divided into parts, a ready environment for bureaucracy. Even the architecture of the college campus was determined by the Cartesian-Newtonian paradigm, with a separate building for each area of college life: dormitories for sleeping, dining halls for eating, chapels for worship, admissions buildings for student recruitment, and so on. The end result was separation, isolation, and poor communication; students were forced to find their own ways of overcoming.

In summary, having cut themselves off from the influence of the church and becoming increasingly influenced by the public university, many church-related colleges lost their unique identity and mission. They patterned themselves academically and administratively after the separation and isolation of the Cartesian-Newtonian paradigm. They "bought" the notion of value-free education. As a result, there was less to distinguish the church-related college from the public university. The church-related college lost its historic *raison d'être*. Faith lost its unifying and energizing influence. These colleges also lost their historic touchstone—the church—so that there was little to call them back to their unique identity and mission. In this vacuum, the secular winds within America also blew into the church-related colleges. The colleges lost their opportunity to be a unique voice within American higher education and to address the crisis in meaning which currently plagues American society.

THE MAINLINE PROTESTANT DENOMINATIONS

Like the church-related colleges, the mainline Protestant denominations are in captivity. They have been under the heady influence of the public universities since the Second World War and have accepted the Cartesian-Newtonian paradigm as if it were reality. When did you last hear the mainline Protestant denominations criticize the public university or critique its underlying philosophy? The church has engaged itself in critical analysis of other parts of our culture, including business and government. But it has not distanced itself far enough from the public university to be critical. In this sense the mainline Protestant denominations have become captives of the public university.

Before World War II, the clergy were products of their respective church-related colleges. Now most of the clergy in the mainline Protestant denominations are graduates of the public universities. Many of the lay members of the mainline Protestant denominations are also graduates of the public universities. These universities gave clergy and laity alike their education and therefore their credentials. How is the church to obtain a critical perspective under these conditions?

The public universities are the most powerful, most influential institutions in America; they have replaced the church in influence. Yet the church has not recognized the far-reaching way in which the public university has been shaping American life.

Nor has the church been able to differentiate its own values and message from the point of view and values of the public university. The silence of the church is evidence of its captivity.

Because the mainline Protestant denominations have been under the powerful influence of the public universities, they have also been under the influence of the Cartesian-Newtonian paradigm. This is true not just in the sense of accepting the general climate in which we live; after the Second World War the mainline Protestant denominations began to organize congregational life, programs, and clergy into specialties. The denominations developed ministers of preaching, ministers of calling, ministers of education, and ministers of counseling. Theology, too, was broken up into specialties (e.g., biblical theology, liberation theology, feminist theology). Clergy specialized in a particular form of ministry: urban ministry, rural ministry, campus ministry, prison ministry, or singles' ministry, to name the more common. The life and missions of the church, under the influence of the Cartesian-Newtonian paradigm, were broken up into parts just as much as the public university.

In an earlier chapter I made reference to the difficult task which theologians faced, working as they did within the Cartesian-Newtonian paradigm. The church's response was to focus on ethics more than on theology. The church and the university became bedfellows in their concentration on social ethics after World War II. Reinhold Niebuhr became the focus of attention, the guru of the mainline Protestant denominations. Theology waned; ethics flourished.

While it seemed to be an appropriate response by the church to the burgeoning student population at the public university, campus ministry—in hindsight—was forced to fit into the Cartesian-Newtonian paradigm which reigned supreme in the public university. Campus ministry was simply another specialty that had to find its niche alongside the other disciplines— even though it had to be based outside the organization of the university. But it was difficult to flourish in an environment which essentially denies transcendence. After functioning in this unfortunate climate for several decades, in recent years campus ministry has shown its weariness. While the mainline Protestant denominations should be applauded for their effort to respond to the large student population which flocked to the public university, it is nevertheless unfortunate that this ministry of the mainline Protestant denominations was based on terms dictated by the public university. In accommodating itself to this second-class citizenship, the church did not do itself a service.

In earlier chapters I chronicled how distance was placed between the mainline Protestant denominations and their colleges. Often both sides wanted this distance, primarily because both accepted the notion of the value-free approach to higher education. Frank Newman points out that "to proclaim to students that the campus is neutral toward ideas is itself to propose a profound value system."[28] George Buttrick puts it even more forcefully: "One of the sorriest assumptions of secular education is its assumption that it makes no assumptions. Actually it makes one whacking assumption—that all life is secular."[29] This myth was perpetrated upon college and church alike. The result is that many church-related colleges traded Christian assumptions for secular assumptions about life and thus became proponents of a secular view of life.

The mainline Protestant denominations bear part of the responsibility for the fact that many of their colleges lost their *raison d'être*. The church was no longer a friendly critic who could and would ask tough questions of their colleges; the church had no prophetic distance from which these questions would arise. Similarly, the church also lost a friendly critic, one familiar with the church's mission and goals. The church also lost a source of enrichment for its own culture. It was easier for the church to become a captive of the public university when it was distanced from its own colleges, and when these colleges no longer had anything truly unique (other than smallness) to offer church or culture. In the post-war years, both the church and its colleges

28. Frank Newman, *Higher Education and American Resurgence* (Washington, DC: The Carnegie Foundation for the Advancement of Teaching, 1985), p. 59.
29. In Lowry, p. 77.

lost their way under the dominance of the public university. Both church and college are the poorer as a result.

The mainline Protestant denominations must confront some tough questions. What kind of prophetic voice can the church have when it is itself held captive within an alien world-view? Can the church—led by people trained in the public university—get any distance from the culture in which it lives in order to be prophetic? Can the church get out from under the influence of the Cartesian-Newtonian paradigm in order to do theology in a new, free atmosphere? Recovering from the Cartesian-Newtonian paradigm, will the church regain its proper grounding in theology and therefore regain its vision, strength, and influence in American society, including within higher education?

And will the church be of any assistance in helping the church-related college find a new, revitalized *raison d'être?* We are in a shakedown era in higher education. Now is the time for tough questions—for the public university, the church-related college, and the mainline Protestant denominations. Now is the time for the church-related college to rediscover its history, its identity, its mission. Now is the time for the church-related college to develop a new *raison d'être.*

II. Toward a New *Raison d'Être* for the Church-Related College

5. Christian Tenets and the Church-Related College

The next three chapters will contain my view of the future direction which the church-related colleges should take, the foundation stones on which they should build. In this chapter we will discuss how Christian tenets should shape the church-related college.

HISTORICAL BACKGROUND

The Christian faith inherited its great interest and involvement in education from its Hebrew and Jewish roots, particularly from the synagogue. The synagogue was the setting for systematic instruction in knowing the law of God and in regulating life according to God's commandments. From earliest times the Jewish community had been dedicated to learning.

Christianity adopted the same attitude toward education. The early churches emphasized gaining adherents to the new faith, but it was also important to instruct new catechumens in the faith. As the Christian faith spread from Jewish soil to the Greco-Roman world, the church incorporated much of the Greek and Roman understanding of education. The Greek world emphasized grammar, rhetoric, and logic (the trivium), and the Roman world emphasized arithmetic, geometry, music, and astronomy (the quadrivium). The early church father Augustine thought that the human intellect was needed to understand the ways of God. The human mind and human culture were God-given attributes which, when cultivated, would bring mankind to understand better the ways of God. Like Augustine, Jerome and Ambrose also believed that human learning would enhance the Christian life.

In the Middle Ages, the trivium and the quadrivium were the basic studies, informed by theology as Christianity took control of the intellectual world of Europe. The late Middle Ages saw the founding of great universities, all under the influence of the church. By the late Middle Ages, the church had found its thought process and therefore its destiny within the liberal arts. The liberal arts helped the church to reason validly and therefore give internal soundness to the faith. And since the ambience of faith was human culture, the church saw that its point of view was best advanced when it understood and used the best of human culture and learning. Theology, the queen of the sciences, helped to pursue the origin and destiny of man—eternal matters—while the other liberal arts enriched human understanding of faith and temporal life. Education, therefore, was seen as indispensable to this life and the next.

The Reformation only served to heighten the church's interest in and promotion of education. One of the major tenets of Protestantism was the priesthood of all believers, with the concomitant notion that all persons should have the right and ability to interpret Scripture for themselves. These two related principles assumed an educated laity as well as clergy. The Reformation was also heir to the Renaissance, the European cultural flowering which infused the Reformation with an appreciation of the liberal arts.

John Calvin was a humanist and theologian who was greatly indebted to the Renaissance. He believed that human culture was part of God's creation and should be accepted and appreciated as such. In his *Institutes of the Christian Religion,* Calvin attempted to give an organized and comprehensive explanation of the Christian faith. In so doing, he drew heavily upon his own scholarly training in the humanities, as well as on theology. Calvin promoted the establishment of schools, as his followers have done ever since.

Martin Luther was one of the leading champions of the idea that the common person should have the right and ability to interpret Scripture. He translated the Bible into the vernacular so that it could be read by the common person, and he also wrote catechisms so that the common person could have an intellectual understanding of the faith. A professor himself, Luther held that schools were second in importance only to the church.

The American colonies were established by people who stood firmly in the tradition of the Reformation, including its emphasis upon education. Less than one hundred years elapsed from the time of Calvin to the founding of Harvard in the 1630s. The Puritans had barely arrived when they established a college, so deeply entrenched had the importance of education already become. And it is important to note the connection between the Protestant understanding of the Christian faith and education. Faith could not thrive without being supported and embellished by education; no education was acceptable if it was not permeated by the Christian faith. In the colonial colleges, faith and learning were not only suitable for each other, they were totally intertwined.

Like the colonial colleges, the frontier colleges of the mainline Protestant denominations integrated faith and learning. The founders of these colleges, usually members of some European ethnic group, sought to perpetuate their faith, values, and piety in their new surroundings. They needed to provide civil and professional leadership for their communities as well as a trained clergy for their churches. Thus, they stood firmly in the Reformation tradition as they established colleges in their frontier communities almost immediately.

It would be misleading to picture these colleges as models of perfection in integrating faith and learning. Some pursued faith at the expense of learning, believing that faith was threatened by learning. Others pursued learning at the expense of faith, believing that learning was diminished by faith. But generally, until the Second World War, the church-related colleges played out the traditional notion that faith and learning could and should be integrated. Indeed, the historic purpose of the church-related college was to integrate faith and learning.

This traditional integration of faith and learning was all but destroyed after World War II. With the spread of pluralism and secularism, there was explosive growth in the large public universities, and the increasing dominance of the Cartesian-Newtonian paradigm, the value-free approach to education came to dominate the universities and the church-related colleges. The ill effects of this were sketched in chapter 3.

THE CHURCH AND HIGHER EDUCATION

Historically, the church has been involved in higher education and this involvement must continue. Higher education is the chief marketplace where worldviews, values, and ideas are discussed, shaped, and appropriated. Silence from the church within the chief marketplace of ideas is an abdication of responsibility. An easy acceptance of the prevailing point of view within higher education by the church suggests that the church is captive to our culture. To be duped into thinking that higher education is somehow neutral is a continuing tragedy. To believe that starting from Christian assumptions is somehow less desirable or wrong is to fall prey to our secular society. To be timid about offering an education built upon Christian tenets is to succumb to the influence of secularism and the value-free myth.

The church must bring a more critical eye and prophetic voice to higher education than it has done during the past four decades, and throw off the domination of the public university. The church must cut through the fuzzy thinking and the erroneous mythology so prevalent in our society. Like much of American society, it has been enamored with the university and therefore under its spell. The church must pull away from the domination of the university and regain its own perspective. Our times call for a prophetic voice from the church in higher education. To withhold this prophetic voice is to abdicate responsibility and to miss opportunity.

The church should recreate its relationship with its colleges, making sure that these colleges are not simply small versions of the universities, but rather colleges which build their total educational enterprise on Christian assumptions and the major Christian tenets. Through the church-related colleges, the mainline Protestant denominations can be a prophetic voice in higher education and in American society in general, and offer an alternative worldview, value system, and educational experience based upon Christian tenets and assumptions, instead of a secular experience based upon the Cartesian-Newtonian paradigm. These church-related colleges will in turn help to articulate the church's voice, as well as enriching its culture. There is an urgency in American society and in the church for a revitalized and redirected church-related college.

Church-related colleges have taken two basic approaches toward their mission. The first, founded on basic Christian doctrines, is that the church ought to promote the liberal arts for their own sake. Human knowledge and intellectual activity are God-given capacities, and therefore the church ought to help enrich human life and society by promoting the liberal arts through education. The skills involved in rational thought are also God-given skills which lift the human to a greater understanding and enjoyment of the creation and human culture. Following Aristotle's lead, proponents of this position maintain that the church ought to promote the "intellectual virtues," namely, art, science, intuition, reasoning, and practical wisdom. The rationale for the church's involvement in liberal arts colleges is the promotion of the intrinsic worth of these intellectual virtues.

The second position is that the church should promote these "intellectual virtues" along with the "moral virtues." The two should be inseparable. Indeed, the moral virtues should direct and provide the right ethos for the intellectual virtues. This second position holds that moral direction must not be separated from the pursuit of the liberal arts. Surely the church is right to assist students in developing their intellectual skills and in acquiring the broadest possible scope of human knowledge. But this goal is in itself too limited. Intellectual knowledge and skills must be given a moral context. The church-related college must

89

be engaged in the pursuit of both the intellectual virtues *and* the moral virtues. Indeed, contemporary American society is too often characterized by a lack of moral judgment and direction. If the church-related college pursues only the intellectual virtues, it pursues only part of our God-given possibility and responsibility; the whole person must be developed.

The church-related college must not be a party to the current attitude in American society and in the public university which claims that education ought not try to influence an individual's faith or morality. Also to be resisted is the separation of knowledge into parts, with knowledge left to specialists who are competent only in their narrow fields and who therefore leave moral, ethical, and spiritual issues to other specialists. The public university, with its current secular and value-free focus, must not be the model for the church-related college. The secular winds blowing in American society must not determine the nature and purpose of the church-related college. The church-related college is private so that it can pursue the moral virtues and provide American society with a distinctive and all-important alternative approach to higher education. The church-related college must regain its unique purpose and mission and provide American society with an educational enterprise that pursues the intellectual and moral virtues in an integrated way.

THEOLOGICAL UNDERPINNINGS FOR THE CHURCH-RELATED COLLEGE

Church-related colleges should build their educational enterprise upon a number of major Christian tenets. The following list is illustrative rather than exhaustive.

One Christian tenet that should shape the church-related college is the doctrine of creation. The created order is the result of the imagination and work of the transcendent, loving God. "In the beginning God created . . ." (Gen. 1:1). A number of important points flow from this position.

The doctrine of creation is supported by the doctrine of incarnation in asserting that the church identify itself with the liberal arts and sciences. Both doctrines demand from us a positive view of and involvement in the created order and human culture. God honored creation by himself becoming man in Jesus Christ. The church is involved in promoting the liberal arts and sciences because human knowledge and human intellectual activity are God-given, God-created capacities, and they should be used to enrich human life and society. Rational thought involves God-given skills which lift the person to a greater understanding and enjoyment of God, creation, and human culture.

Following Aristotle's lead, the church promotes these "intellectual virtues." But the church also promotes what Aristotle called the "moral virtues." The moral virtues involve a person's value system, worldview, and ethical system. The moral virtues provide the framework for a person's life and the ambience for the intellectual virtues. Indeed, the moral virtues direct the intellectual virtues, and give knowledge and skills a moral context in which to function. The church-related college should educate young people not only in the intellectual virtues, but in the moral virtues as well.

It should be obvious that the doctrine of creation established the concept of the transcendence of God. Thus, while a secular education, especially one under the domination of the Cartesian-Newtonian paradigm, denies transcendence, the church-related college *begins* with the concept of transcendence. Transcendence is the starting point. The doctrine of creation rightly sends the church-related college down an altogether different track than an educational approach which denies transcendence.

The doctrine of creation also describes a holistic or unified created order rather than a dualistic order which divides all creation into the good and the bad. At the conclusion of creation, God looked upon all that he had created and pronounced it good (Gen. 1:31). The purpose of the writer of Genesis was to establish a positive attitude toward creation. The doctrine of incarnation only serves to confirm this positive attitude toward the created order. "God so loved the world, that he gave his only begotten Son" (John 3:16). Thus, the church-related college should deny dualism in whatever form it takes and promote the goodness of the created order.

Nor is life split up into parts at its most elementary level as the Cartesian-Newtonian paradigm contends. The doctrine of creation holds to a unity, a connectedness, in the created order. Thus the church-related college must, on theological grounds, deny the Cartesian-Newtonian paradigm which separates and isolates creation into many parts. The church-related college should develop its educational enterprise on the basis of the unity of creation, the connectedness of all matter. The created order was given this unity by its Creator.

The doctrine of creation also urges the church-related college to be involved not only in the investigation of the created order and the transmission of this knowledge through the liberal arts, but also to be involved in human society. The church-related college is not called to separate itself from human society but rather to live by Christian values within society so as to witness to and thus transform society. Here the church-related college associated with the mainline Protestant denominations is at odds with some of her sister colleges in the fundamentalist tradition who wish to separate themselves from human society in an "otherworldly" stance.

The doctrines of sin and salvation give the church-related college a unique point of view in the world of higher education. On the one hand, the church-related college points to and attempts to enrich the high status and capabilities of man suggested in the Bible: we are created in the image of God. But in the midst of this high position the Bible also points out the role that sin plays in human existence. This tension between the high value and capability of mankind on the one hand, and the sinfulness of man on the other, should be recognized by the church-related college.

Added to this position, however, are the doctrines of the incarnation, crucifixion, and resurrection of Jesus Christ, which hold out a new life for the person who wishes to appropriate, through faith, God's loving, saving activity. The educational enterprise of the church-related college must take into account both sin and salvation. And while it is not the primary task of the church-related college to proclaim this message in the same way that it is the church's task to do so, nevertheless the worldview of the church-related college must take this viewpoint into consideration. It is important for a church-related college to have a Christian faculty which, in its diversity, points out the Christian viewpoint through faculty members' various disciplines and through its general presence on the campus. Unity or "at-one-ment" must be a goal of the church-related college. The "good news" that new life, a reconciled life with God and with one's fellowman, is available must be part of the viewpoint and message of the church-related college. Enlarging and enriching the lives of persons who have this new life is surely the task of the church-related college. Again, such a stance gives the church-related college a unique identity and mission.

Let me give one final illustration. Contemporary American culture promotes the notion that the goal of life is self-fulfillment; thus it should be the aim of education to assist people toward self-fulfillment. But the doctrine of the church suggests a different goal of life and of education. The Christian faith calls its adherents not to self-fulfillment (admirable as that concept is), but rather to discipleship under the Lordship of Christ. We are called to obedience. We are called to seek the will of God, not our own wills. Therefore the church-related college should point its students not toward self-fulfillment, as our culture desires, but rather toward living their lives to the glory of God through discipleship.

While these are only a few examples, they should suffice to point out that the church-related college should base its enterprise on Christian tenets. And it should be obvious that basing its identity and mission on Christian tenets will give it a unique point of view.

At all cost, the mainline Protestant denominations and their church-related colleges must avoid refining these major tenets into minute detail. Such an approach leads to sectarianism and sectarianism leads to divisiveness. It was this divisiveness which in earlier decades encouraged the value-free approach to education. While individual denominations are free to develop a unique ethos on their college campuses, it should not be at the expense of a broad unity based upon the major Christian tenets. Without unity, the church-related colleges will make little impact on American society or on higher education. Without unity these colleges will not offer a viable alternative to our society. The colleges affiliated with the mainline Protestant denominations must strive for a common, unified, and easily recognizable alternative to the secular educational enterprise which has become the dominant force in American higher education.

An educational enterprise based on the major Christian tenets will not only give the students at these church-related colleges the right worldview, but it will also give higher education something which the critics are saying is missing in current higher education: integration and coherence. Ernest L. Boyer says that colleges have an obligation "to give students a sense of passage toward a more coherent view of knowledge and a more integrated life."[1] A study done by Lutheran educators challenges church-related colleges to respond to this need for integration:

> Are we giving all students a consciousness of the unity of learning and the organization of truth within a Christian outlook? . . . We know that in secular universities either a naturalistic or an idealistic theory of education, or at least an indifference to religion in education, is apparent. What does it mean for us to make religion central? Unless the Christian college is providing a leadership that can see life steadily and see it whole within a philosophy of education that makes Christ and His truth central, we are yielding by default to pagan philosophies and secularization.
>
> It should be apparent now why the church has such a stake in liberal education. It is here where the battle of ideas is joined. . . . It is in the humanities, the social sciences, and the natural sciences that a Christian philosophy can and does make a tremendous difference, and where the Christian Church must combat pagan philosophies of culture.[2]

Arthur F. Holmes points out that the large secular universities are not universities but rather "multiversities," institutions without a unifying worldview and therefore without unifying

1. Boyer, *College,* p. 68.
2. Harold H. Ditmanson, Howard V. Hong, and Warren A. Quanbeck, eds., *Christian Faith and the Liberal Arts* (Minneapolis: Augsburg, 1960), p. 31.

educational goals. By contrast, the church-related college, because it refuses to compartmentalize religion, retains the unifying Christian worldview.[3]

Frank Newman points to the urgency of providing students with such an integrated experience in which they confront and wrestle with ultimate value issues:

> The College years are ones of special significance. Students begin their life away from their families. They begin to vote. It is a time of shift from the narrowly held views of adolescence to the more reasoned views of adulthood. It is a time when students are led into a larger view of the moral problems and decisions, and a time when they learn to move from the abstractions of moral theory to the dilemmas of moral action. The values that are developed at this time in their lives will persist throughout life.[4]

Nels Ferré said it well several decades ago: "If the Christian faith is understood in its deepest and widest nature, nothing hinders its becoming central to higher education. False theologies, ignorance, and fear are the real deterrents that debar the Christian faith from its natural place at the center of both the thought and life of higher education."[5] The point of view of the 1960 Lutheran study is similar:

> Today the Christian liberal arts college is a very necessary arm of the church in the church's never-ending battle against the secularization of life. The Christian liberal arts colleges of our church are a standing testimony to the church's concern for the best culture of its members, a learning that is to be gained within a true community of scholars with a common mission and a learning that is integrated within the context of a Christian outlook on life and knowledge.[6]

The church must be involved in higher education, to provide a Christian worldview that will counter the prevailing secu-

---

3. Arthur F. Holmes, *The Idea of a Christian College,* rev. ed. (Grand Rapids: Eerdmans, 1987), p. 9.

4. Newman, p. 58.

5. Nels S. F. Ferré, *Christian Faith and Higher Education* (New York: Harper and Brothers, 1954), p. 123.

6. Ditmanson, Hong, and Quanbeck, p. 32.

lar one in our society and particularly in higher education. The church must also provide students with a unified, integrated educational experience, one that is based upon a Christian worldview in place of the separated, fragmented approach to education which typifies much of American higher education. To do this, the church-related college must offer an educational enterprise based upon Christian tenets.

6. The Post-Modern Science Paradigm

Most of us are accustomed to the notion that the world is just as we perceive it. But as has been pointed out in earlier chapters, what we see and what we believe depends upon the paradigm within which we operate. A paradigm provides us with a pair of glasses, as it were. What we view as reality is seen through these glasses. A paradigm is a viewpoint, a mindset, a particular bias held in common, or a shared consciousness. It is an *estimate* of reality, a belief about how things are, a shared set of assumptions.

The paradigm under which the Western world has lived for approximately four centuries was first shaped by Descartes and Newton. It was the paradigm which allowed science to flourish. According to this paradigm, the world is basically a closed, completed, and unchanging system. While Descartes and Newton believed in God, they ruled out any activity on God's part in this machinelike world. Following Descartes and Newton, many scientists and philosophers ruled out transcendence altogether because it was not verifiable. Actually this paradigm became more than a paradigm; it became a metaphysical world-view.

Since the late nineteenth and early twentieth centuries, some physicists and mathematicians have carried out experiments and developed theories which simply will not fit within the confines of the Cartesian-Newtonian paradigm. These scientists include Emil Wiechert, Niels Bohr, Ernest Rutherford, Kurt Gödel, Michael

Polanyi, and John Wheeler—not exactly household names. It is very difficult to develop a new paradigm. Most scientists tend to force their theories and the results of their experiments into the established paradigm. For example, it has just become public knowledge that Newton held, but suppressed, a much more open and integrated view of the universe.[1] Even Einstein forced his theories to fit into the old paradigm.[2]

Currently, scientists divide themselves into two camps. Many are still working at fitting all theories into the old paradigm, believing that the world is a mathematical package that can and will be understood by one unified package of theories. Others believe that the Cartesian-Newtonian paradigm is inaccurate. Instead of seeing a universe that is closed, knowable, and predictable, their world is open, infinite, and subject to random, unpredictable developments. Contrary to the earlier belief that each bit of matter is separate and independent, this new view holds that everything is connected and interrelated.

Freeman Dyson writes: "My own field of physics is passing today through a phase of exuberant freedom, a phase of passionate prodigality."[3] This freedom is in sharp contrast to the domination of the Cartesian-Newtonian paradigm. Dyson points out that when matter is examined in its finest detail, its actions are *un*predictable. Dyson then observes: "We stand, in a manner of speaking, midway between the unpredictability of matter and the unpredictability of God."[4] The world of those scientists who are shaping the post-modern science paradigm is radically different from the world of the scientists of the Cartesian-Newtonian paradigm. The world of the new paradigm is open, alive, and surprising. Dyson takes the title of his book, *Infinite in All Directions,* from an address by one of the earliest proponents of a new paradigm, Emil Wiechert. In 1896, Wiechert said:

1. Freeman J. Dyson, *Infinite in All Directions: An Exploration of Science and Religion* (New York: Harper & Row, 1988), p. 50.
2. *Ibid.,* p. 7.
3. *Ibid.,* p. 6.
4. *Ibid.,* p. 8.

So far as modern science is concerned, we have to abandon completely the idea that by going into the realm of the small we shall reach the ultimate foundations of the universe. I believe we can abandon this idea without any regret. The universe is infinite in all directions, not only above us in the large but also below us in the small.[5]

In place of the completed, machinelike universe, Freeman Dyson paints a different picture, one of diversity:

The discoveries of recent decades in particle physics have led us to place great emphasis on the concept of broken symmetry. The development of the universe from its earliest beginnings is regarded as a succession of symmetry-breakings. As it emerges from the moment of creation in the Big Bang, the universe is completely symmetrical and featureless. As it cools to lower and lower temperatures, it breaks one symmetry after another, allowing more and more diversity of structure to come into existence. The phenomenon of life also fits naturally into this picture. Life too is a symmetry-breaking. In the beginning a homogeneous ocean somehow differentiated itself into cells and animalcules, predators and prey. Later on, a homogeneous population of apes differentiated itself into languages and cultures, arts and sciences and religions. Every time a symmetry is broken, new levels of diversity and creativity become possible. It may be that the nature of our universe and the nature of life are such that this process of diversification will have no end.[6]

Not only does the post-modern science paradigm emphasize openness and diversity, it reintroduces awe and mystery. While it does not demand transcendence, it allows, perhaps even suggests, transcendence. At least it creates a climate where faith and science can live harmoniously side by side, each playing an integral role in the life of humankind. The new paradigm certainly rejects the reductionist view that only that which is verifiable is real.

The post-modern science paradigm continues to look at the

5. Quoted in *ibid.,* p. 36.
6. *Ibid.,* pp. 43-44.

minute parts of nature, but instead of holding that life at its most basic can be broken down into parts, the post-modern science paradigm emphasizes integration and wholeness, interdependence and connectedness. The most basic picture of our world is relatedness. Thus the post-modern science paradigm breaks with the Cartesian-Newtonian paradigm and offers a new pattern within which to perceive our world and develop theories and beliefs.

Perhaps the best way to attempt to understand the new paradigm—the paradigm of post-modern science—is to see it in juxtaposition to the Cartesian-Newtonian paradigm. These two ways of looking at reality differ at four major points:

1. *Knowing versus inferring:* While according to the Cartesian-Newtonian paradigm the physical world is the basic reality and is completely knowable, under the post-modern science paradigm the "world-in-itself" is *not* knowable; only our interaction with the physical world-in-itself is knowable. Our knowledge of the world-in-itself comes only from inference.

2. *Individual elements versus systems:* The Cartesian-Newtonian paradigm contends that the physical world is made up of basic entities with distinct properties distinguishing one element from another. Isolating and reducing the physical world to its most basic entities, its separate parts, provides us with a completely knowable, predictable, and therefore controllable physical universe. In contrast, the post-modern science paradigm holds that the scientist deals in interactions rather than separate entities. At its most basic level, the world is connected and interdependent.

3. *Space and time versus space-time:* The Cartesian-Newtonian paradigm contends that space is passive, that it exists in its own right and holds all of the objects of the physical world. Likewise, time exists in its own right and flows independently and inexorably. In contrast, within the post-modern science paradigm neither space nor time exists independently in its own right, but both are inseparably bound together in a four-dimensional space-time.

4. *Certainty and finality versus probability and creativity:* The Cartesian-Newtonian paradigm contends that the physical

universe is governed by immutable laws and therefore is determined and predictable, like an enormous machine. In principle, knowledge of the world could be complete in all its details. In contrast, under the post-modern science paradigm uncertainty is basic to our understanding of the universe; uncertainty has ontological status. Probability is as close as we can come to predicting outcomes. Beyond the historic categories in logic of true and false, there exists another category—the undecidable— thus making reality open.[7]

At the turn of the century, it was becoming increasingly clear to more and more scientists that the Cartesian-Newtonian paradigm was inadequate, that it had been forcing reality into its mold for a long time and that reality could not be held in this paradigm any longer. A new paradigm was necessary; indeed, this new paradigm has been developing for almost a century.

Just as the Cartesian-Newtonian paradigm had its origin in the natural sciences, particularly physics and mathematics, so did this new paradigm. And just as the Cartesian-Newtonian paradigm provided the glasses or worldview for the entire population of the Western world, so will the new post-modern science paradigm. The implications of this change in paradigms are far-reaching—for society in general, for the church, and for the church-related college. While we should be grateful for all of the good which the Cartesian-Newtonian paradigm did for and brought to the Western world, we can at the same time be grateful that our worldview can now change to one in which connectedness is basic, life is properly viewed as related systems, and the universe is open to transcendence, mystery, and awe. The new paradigm is helping us to get away from what Alfred North Whitehead called the "misplaced

7. For further reading see: John Gribbin, *In Search of Schrodinger's Cat: Quantum Physics and Reality* (New York: Bantam Books, 1984); Freeman J. Dyson, *Infinite in All Directions* (New York: Harper & Row, 1988); Ian G. Barbour, *Issues in Science and Religion* (Englewood Cliffs, NJ: Prentice-Hall, 1966); Ian G. Barbour, *Myths, Models and Paradigms* (New York: Harper & Row, 1974); Howard K. Schilling, *The New Consciousness in Science and Religion* (Philadelphia: United Church Press, 1973); Thomas S. Kuhn, *The Structure of Scientific Revolutions* (Chicago: University of Chicago Press, 1962); Michael Polanyi, *Personal Knowledge* (Chicago: University of Chicago Press, 1958).

concreteness" of focusing on parts and things rather than on relationships.

Two major dimensions of the post-modern science paradigm in particular hold a great deal of promise. The first is that, while reality can be *broken* up into parts, at its most basic life is connected; life is interrelated and whole. Life is basically a system. John Gribbin writes:

> Virtually everything we see and touch and feel is made up of collections of particles right back through time, to the Big Bang in which the universe as we know it came into being. The atoms in my body are made of particles that once jostled in close proximity in the cosmic fireball with particles that are from the body of some living creature on some distant, undiscovered planet. Indeed, the particles that make up my body once jostled in close proximity and interacted with the particles that now make up your body.[8]

Along a similar vein, but using a different metaphor, Schilling comments:

> Contemporary man can now sense the symphonic character of physical reality and hear metaphorically the music of the spheres within the atom. He is far more fascinated by the melodic quality and dynamism of its singing than by the blueprints of its mechanical structure.[9]

The second major feature of the post-modern science paradigm is that it has a more *inclusive* view of reality. The new paradigm incorporates the human mind and consciousness as well as human spirit, whereas for all practical purposes these entities were ignored by the Cartesian-Newtonian paradigm. Thus, a whole new arena of consideration has been opened up, one which takes seriously man in his wholeness. In this atmosphere, religion can have a much more positive place. If the old paradigm was deterministic, flat, and closed, the new paradigm is open, dynamic, and creative. Benjamin A. Reist writes:

8. Gribbin, *Schrodinger's Cat*, pp. 229-30.
9. Schilling, *New Consciousness*, p. 82.

The Christian tradition . . . has always insisted that God is alive. Perhaps we can now grasp this in utterly unforeseen ways, and thus find even deeper reaches in the term "faith" than have so far been discerned.[10]

Schilling points out that one of the fundamental qualities of reality, viewed through the prism of the post-modern science paradigm, is its mystery. "Mystery" here does *not* mean an as-yet-unsolved problem or puzzle, or a gap in our knowledge, as in the Cartesian-Newtonian position; rather, mystery in the post-modern science paradigm refers to the unknowable, incomprehensible, inexplicable, or even inaccessible. Furthermore, nature is mysterious because what is known evokes endless wonder and awe.[11]

IMPLICATIONS FOR SOCIETY, CHURCH, AND COLLEGE

Just as the Cartesian-Newtonian paradigm reached into every segment of society, so the post-modern science paradigm has the opportunity to have a profound and far-reaching influence upon society.

Regaining the possibility of transcendence could be one of the most important results of this change of paradigms. Whereas the Cartesian-Newtonian paradigm created an environment and mindset in which it was difficult to include transcendence, the post-modern science paradigm takes the lid off the universe, as it were, and opens up the mind, the imagination, and the spirit of our consciousness. However, we must be careful not to imagine that the new paradigm says more than it really does, lest we follow the pendulum too far in the opposite direction. In no way does the new paradigm offer new proofs for God. Nor should we allow it to become a new metaphysical system. But it does do something massively im-

10. Benjamin A. Reist, "New Theological Horizons in the Light of Post-Modern Science," *Pacific Theological Review* (Spring 1985): 10.
11. Schilling, pp. 30-31.

portant: it creates a worldview that includes transcendence. It allows for a transcendent God who is alive and active in our world. Whereas the Cartesian-Newtonian paradigm tended to curtail—if not completely negate—transcendence and the possibility of a God active in the physical universe, the postmodern science paradigm opens up these possibilities. A whole new atmosphere is possible in society.

With the recovery of the possibility of transcendence comes the possibility of a sense of transcendent authority. In the first chapter we mentioned "Margaret," one of Robert Bellah's interviewees, who believed whatever moral authority there was existed within herself. With this new paradigm, society can now attempt to develop some sense of communal authority with a transcendent base, instead of basing moral authority upon what each individual person feels is right.

Our society, so materialistic as the result of the emphasis upon the "here and now" of the Cartesian-Newtonian paradigm, can perhaps begin to see that the realm of the human spirit is real, and that it needs to commune with the divine, as so many young people in the 1960s sought to do through Eastern religions. Our society may begin to see that amassing and consuming goods is not the main purpose of life. Christians may be put back in touch with Christendom's own tradition of spirituality, which has been all but forgotten. Technology, which has admittedly been very beneficial to society, may be balanced with an increased emphasis upon the humanities and the arts.

The focus on the individual at the expense of the community may now be questioned. Perhaps we will see how important the group is to the health of the individual and attempt to value the group more. The concept of individuation and the resulting isolation which developed out of the Cartesian-Newtonian paradigm has had a negative impact upon society. We have elevated the individual and individual needs at the expense of the group, whether that group be the married couple, family, or community. The result has been isolation and loneliness for the person and an undernourished group. We have lost connectedness; we have not nurtured our historic linkages of family and community, and thus we have lost the wholeness, caring, and healing that community offers the individual. But with this new model of integration there can be a new emphasis upon this very necessary feature of humanity.

Whereas the Cartesian-Newtonian paradigm led to the *use* of people through management techniques, the new paradigm can bring a new emphasis upon the importance and value of the individual. The machine should not be our model of how society works; our model should be the organism or ecosystem. A person is not replaceable like a part in a machine, but rather each person is an invaluable dimension of the system.

A new approach to the care of the earth can also come from a move away from viewing the world as machinelike. Under the Cartesian-Newtonian worldview, the earth's resources are meant for the machine, and the machine has intrinsic value. In the post-modern science paradigm, the earth's resources are of importance in themselves, as part of the overall system of the universe. People are put into a different value relationship with the rest of the created order. No one dimension of the created order can be harmed without harming the whole. And this connectedness among the various dimensions of the earth can be a model for worldwide human interaction. The possibility of a new model for universal human interaction could not be coming at a more opportune moment in history. Listen to Karl Jaspers:

> What is historically new and, for the first time in history, decisive about our situation is the real unity of mankind on the earth. The planet has become for men a single whole. . . . From our vantage point, the interlude of previous history has the appearance of an area scattered with mutually independent endeavors, as the multiple origin of the potentialities of man. Now the whole world has become the problem and task. With this a total metamorphosis of history has taken place. . . . All the crucial problems have become world problems, the situation a situation of mankind. . . . Nothing essen-

tial can happen anywhere that does not concern all. . . . Technology has brought about the unification of the globe by making possible a hitherto unheard of speed of communications. The history of the one humanity has begun. A single destiny governs the whole.[12]

Perhaps the most profound impact of the post-modern paradigm is that it restores in the human community the concept of vision, of looking beyond a limited horizon, of continuing to look into a microscope, but also letting mankind's imagination soar and dream. The post-modern science paradigm takes the lid off. It gives humankind the opportunity to dream both "micro-dreams" within the physical order as we now see it, and to dream "macro-dreams"; that is, we can follow in the path of the imagination of the transcendent God.

What are the implications of the post-modern science paradigm for the mainline Protestant denominations? All churches, not just the mainline Protestant denominations, will be working in a more positive, promising environment as society comes to live more and more under the influence of the post-modern science paradigm. If the old paradigm was deterministic, flat, and closed, the new paradigm is open, dynamic, and creative. Listen once again to Benjamin A. Reist: "The Christian tradition . . . has always insisted that God is alive. Perhaps we can now grasp this in utterly unforeseen ways, and thus find even deeper reaches in the term 'faith' than have so far been discerned."[13] If secularism does not lose the fertile ground in which it has flourished, then at least the church will have an environment in which faith is a more acceptable concept, in which mystery and awe and the response of worship is more likely.

With the lid off of the old boxed-in worldview and with an entirely new worldview opening up, theology should once again be the lively, if controversial, focus of attention. Theology should again capture the attention of the church; there should be a better balance between theology and ethics. There will be new op-

12. Karl Jaspers, *The Origin and Goal of History* (New Haven: Yale University Press, 1953), pp. 1-3.
13. Reist, p. 10.

portunities and new ways to conceptualize God, within and beyond our physical world. In a more hospitable environment, faith can be integrated with all of the other dimensions of life in a systemic fashion, rather than being merely added on, or even denied altogether.

Under the influence of the Cartesian-Newtonian paradigm and the subsequent loss of mystery and awe, worship has lost its transcendent impetus. Too often liturgy has been watered down until it is no more than a series of unrelated events. Hymnology has become anthropocentric. While congregations have corporately confessed sin, for all practical purposes sin is not a vital concept to many Christians. So-called "self-esteem theology" has attempted to make individual Christians feel better about themselves, but, according to this "theology," the problem is not that they have sinned against God but that they have negative feelings. Instead of focusing on guilt, churches and individual Christians have focused on guilt feelings. And in an atmosphere where members of congregations are not sure that there is transcendence, much less whether God intervenes in human life, the congregational prayer is more for psychological effect than it is an attempt to seek God's intervention. Preaching, that old act of explaining the Scripture and speaking on behalf of God, has become theatrical under the tutelage of television preachers. The post-modern science paradigm gives the church another chance; it provides a chance for a revitalization of worship.

The mainline Protestant denominations have, under the new paradigm, an opportunity to move beyond the corporation as model and beyond management techniques as method. In recent decades the language, if not the agenda, of the church has sounded no different from the language and agenda of the corporation. The mainline Protestant denominations have decentralized, merged, and relocated, activities which have taken up an enormous amount of their attention, energy, and money. A skeptic might ask, to what gain? The mainline Protestant denominations will advance the life and mission of the church more with a vigorous pursuit of theological discussion within the framework of the post-modern science paradigm.

Additional opportunities for change will correct and enrich the life of these denominations. Coupled with the pursuit of theology, these denominations have the opportunity to move in the direction of greater spirituality, to rediscover the literature and practice of meditation and contemplation which have been lost under the influence of the Cartesian-Newtonian paradigm. These churches can also show society the way by pursuing connectedness, integration, and community. They can move beyond the privatism which has crept into faith and correct the unbalanced view of individual salvation which permeates American Christendom.

There is no longer any reason for malaise in the mainline Protestant denominations. They need no longer be in the doldrums and in decline. There is such excitement to be found in breaking out from under the old paradigm and into the new. If the Cartesian-Newtonian paradigm has gripped and stifled Christendom for approximately four hundred years, it need do so no longer. The mainline Protestant denominations only need to let the post-modern science paradigm provide them with the environment in which to flourish.

What about the church-related colleges? By adopting the post-modern science paradigm, the church-related colleges have the opportunity once again to provide leadership for the higher-education enterprise in America. They can once again shape their own model of higher education and offer it to the American public. They can thereby discontinue living according to the model offered by the public university.

To begin with, the church-related colleges can help to educate the public concerning the paradigm by which we currently live, showing the inadequacies of the Cartesian-Newtonian paradigm and how that paradigm has misguided our thinking. The church-related colleges can then demonstrate how the post-modern science paradigm can open up a whole new worldview with its many possibilities and positive implications.

Under the post-modern science paradigm, the church-related colleges can and should reject the reductionist thinking which pervades higher education. They can reject the secular view of life and embrace one that includes the transcendent and accepts the possibility of God's ongoing creative activity within our universe and beyond. This new freedom to see a vast, mysterious universe instead of a closed, machinelike world ought to bring excitement and awe to these church-related colleges, and should encourage new investigative theories and activity.

If the churches have decades of excitement facing them, the church-related colleges ought to be at the front leading the churches. Once again, these colleges ought to model the integration of faith and learning, move faith front and center, and acknowledge that the human being is not a machine but an organism which needs spiritual nourishment and expression. Instead of being value-free, these colleges should take this value stance and offer a unique educational enterprise, one that correctly fits human nature.

Instead of using the Cartesian-Newtonian paradigm of separation and isolation to organize the curriculum, or any other area of college life, the church-related colleges should use the post-modern science paradigm of integration and wholeness to create an interrelated educational program, that interrelation reflected even in the physical facilities. The mission of these colleges ought to be to develop every aspect of the student and to develop wholeness within the student. The residential church-related colleges ought to model community as well, assisting students in connecting with other persons and taking responsibility for them. The church-related colleges ought to be based on the model of the ecosystem rather than the machine.

The church-related colleges ought to train or retrain its faculty to approach their profession differently than most have been trained to do in graduate school. Faculty members should be encouraged to integrate faith and learning, to work in an interdisciplinary fashion with their colleagues, and to treat students as whole persons whose spirits need growth as much as their intellects.

Two additional, related points are necessary at the conclusion of this chapter. First, I have such enthusiasm for the post-modern science paradigm and its implications for both the church and the church-related college, because the concepts of connectedness, integration, and wholeness derived from this paradigm dovetail with the Christian tenets on which I propose that the church-related colleges build their future. These two pillars—the Christian tenets and the post-modern science paradigm—are complementary.

Second, a word of caution is in order. The post-modern science paradigm is just that: a paradigm, a worldview, an *estimate* of reality. We should not make this paradigm into a metaphysical system, as some did with the Cartesian-Newtonian paradigm. In the excitement of the post-modern science paradigm, we must keep in mind that someday this paradigm may prove inadequate; greater truth may someday be known and we must be prepared to move toward that truth. In the meantime, there is much to be done if we are to digest and live creatively with the new vision of reality which the post-modern science paradigm offers.

7. The Seismic Shift in American Culture

We come now to the third pillar for the church-related college. The thesis of this chapter is that, because of the seismic shift in American culture since the Second World War, the mainline Protestant denominations and the church-related colleges must adjust their relationship to American culture; they must take a much more consciously Christian stance.

CHRIST AND CULTURE IN HISTORICAL PERSPECTIVE

When Jesus answered the question about whether or not the Jews should pay taxes, he said: "Render therefore unto Caesar the things which are Caesar's and unto God the things that are God's" (Matt. 22:21). While it may have enlightened the inquirers and while it has told Christians ever since that they have two allegiances, Jesus gave no clear formula for handling these two allegiances. The statement concealed as much—or more—than it revealed.

Reading the gospels (and often reading between the lines), it is clear that Jews living in Palestine gave Caesar some allegiance, but not more than they had to, and they did not do it willingly. After all, they were under Caesar's domination. One of the roles which the synagogue played—within Palestine and throughout the diaspora—was to teach Jews about their tradition, their identity as God's people, and their perceived place in God's scheme of things. While they lived within a civil realm and had to give some allegiance to Caesar, their basic identity as "the people of God" gave them their primary identity and allegiance. Jesus' statement did little more than acknowledge these two allegiances.

The earliest Christians—the ones who lived on Palestinian soil—would have built their lives and found meaning in their identity as the "new Israel." As Christianity spread to the Greco-Roman world, it was natural for Christianity to maintain that same understanding, in part because the entire Greco-Roman world lived under Caesar, and in part because the early Christians continued to stand on the shoulders of the Jews, though they saw themselves as members of "the new covenant."

In his influential book *Christ and Culture,* H. Richard Niebuhr points out that many of the New Testament writers—including Paul, John, and the authors of James, of 1 John, and of Revelation—struggled with this issue, as did many of the early church fathers, including Tertullian, Clement of Alexandria, Justin Martyr, and Marcion. All of these and others attempted to establish a relationship between Christ and culture in the early church. But what is crucial to understand is the *environment* in which they were living and working, the *context* in which they were operating. They lived in an environment which was basically hostile to the Christian faith.

When Constantine, emperor of Rome from 306 to 337 A.D., converted to Christianity and made Christianity the established religion of the Roman Empire, *the context changed.* Suddenly Christianity found itself not persecuted but promoted by "Caesar." The historic position of the synagogue was no longer the position of the church. The synagogue had always been an "alien" in culture, but the church was now on new ground. And under these changed conditions, the statements of Jesus and of the New Testament writers looked different to the church. They appeared in a new light when seen from a different perspective. While this new situation was a much more advantageous position in which to live, it was also a much more ambiguous position from which to determine the relationship between church and culture. Regardless, the church in the

Western world has lived in this friendly relationship with society ever since.

In particular, consider the relationship between church and culture for American mainline Protestant churches. This country was founded largely by persons who were members of the mainline Protestant denominations. The leaders of the United States for the past two hundred years have been either members of or under the influence of the mainline Protestant denominations. Until recently, the leaders in the executive, legislative, and judicial branches of this nation and of its states, generally have been members of the mainline Protestant denominations. Despite the First Amendment, which disallowed the government from establishing, promoting, or favoring a particular religious point of view, this country has been very closely aligned with the Christian faith as expressed in the mainline Protestant denominations. Whether through people (presidents, legislators, or judges), laws (the so-called "blue laws"), mottos ("In God We Trust"), traditions (prayer in the public schools), or through a host of other ways in the workings of our government, the mainline Protestant point of view has been the religious point of view of this society.

It has not been the government alone which has been closely identified with the mainline Protestant denominations. The values, customs, and traditions of this society have been shaped and transmitted by the mainline Protestant denominations, and these denominations created much of American culture as well. The public school system, very much an outgrowth of the emphasis which these denominations placed upon education, has stood right alongside the mainline Protestant churches in teaching American youth the values, customs, and traditions held by these denominations. The very air which America breathes has been that which the mainline Protestant denominations have breathed into this nation since its inception.

In the first half of the twentieth century, the mainline Protestant denominations and American culture (government and society) seemed to fit together like the proverbial "hand-in-glove." Church and culture seemed to pursue the same goals, hold the same values, even (dare I say) serve the same Lord. This

113

should not be surprising in light of the "Manifest Destiny" which permeated American society during and after the nineteenth century. But in the second half of the twentieth century we have seen a distinct change in the American environment, a change which calls into question the historic relationship between the mainline Protestant denominations and American culture.

CHANGES AFTER WORLD WAR II

In his book *Gravity and Grace,* Joseph Sittler writes:

> Ever since the Second World War, there has become obvious in the United States an ever-deepening bewilderment as to the reality of the good, the strength and the persistence of the good: a coarsening of public sensibility toward the problems of personal and national morality, a coarsening of the public hide, as it were. The disastrous war in Vietnam, and the disclosures of the ambiguous character of those in charge of the highest public offices in our land have added to the deepening of moral sensibility that was . . . demanded by the Holocaust, but that has not . . . produced a group of persons in America who are probing . . . into the nature of our human responsibility in reply to the existence of evil.[1]

Referring to the traditional close relationship between the church and American culture, Wade Roof also suggests that a change is taking place in that historic relationship:

> So much a part of the nation's history, religious themes have molded the character of collective life and set the terms for public moral discourse. But some dramatic shifts in these historic patterns have occurred in recent times. There is good reason to believe that the decade of the 1960s was a watershed in American life, and that changes stemming from that time may have substantially altered long-standing relations between religion and culture. . . . By the 1980s the currents of change had rocked virtually all the mainline religious institutions, forcing them to ad-

---

1. Joseph Sittler, *Gravity and Grace: Reflections and Provocations,* ed., Linda-Marie Dellof (Minneapolis: Augsburg, 1986), p. 103.

just to new social realities, to grapple with unprecedented moral challenges, and to seek realignments of power and influence.[2]

Martin Marty referred to the recent changes taking place between mainline Protestant denominations and American culture as a "seismic shift in the nation's religious landscape."[3] In the past, the membership of the mainline Protestant denominations felt that they had a responsibility for the common good of the country, a point of view which Alexis de Tocqueville applauded about early America and which Robert Bellah would like to see continued.

Jack L. Stotts, in a speech delivered as part of a sesquicentennial celebration at Muskingum College, pointed out two changes in the relationship between the mainline Protestant denominations and American culture. The first is the "unresolved nature of the relationship between the mainline churches and the national policies and programs enacted by the state." The second is "the loss of coherence between the motivations, goals and activities of the dominant institutions of the society and the mainline churches."[4]

Even without these two changes, we could note the pluralism which has developed in America after the Second World War and the loss of transcendence and subsequent secularization of American society. Taken together, these four developments have caused changes of seismic proportions on the American scene.

Perhaps the most vivid description of the change in America with which the mainline Protestant churches must come to grips is offered by William H. Willimon:

> Though I could not have known it at the time, a momentous event in my faith journey occurred on a Sunday evening in 1963 in

2. Wade Clark Roof, in preface to *The Annals,* 480 (July 1985): 9.

3. Wade Clark Roof and William McKinney, "Denominational America and the New Religious Pluralism," *The Annals,* 480 (July 1985): 30. (Quoting Martin E. Marty's introduction to Hoge and Roozen, *Understanding Church Growth and Decline.*)

4. Jack L. Stotts, "The Seismic Shift in the Religious Location of Mainline Protestantism" (Paper presented at the sesquicentennial celebration of Muskingum College, New Concord, Ohio, 1987, mimeo.), pp. 3-7.

Greenville, South Carolina, when, in defiance of the state's archaic Blue Laws, the Fox Theater opened on Sunday. Seven of us—regular attenders at the Methodist Youth Fellowship at Buncombe Street Church—made a pact to enter the front door of the church, be seen, then quietly slip out the back door and join John Wayne at the Fox.

Only lately have I come to see how that evening symbolizes a watershed in the history of Christianity in the United States. On that night, Greenville, South Carolina—the last pocket of resistance to secularity in the Western world—gave in and served notice that it would no longer be a prop for the church. If Christians were going to be made in Greenville, then the church must do it alone.

There would be no more free passes for the church, no more free rides. The Fox Theater went head-to-head with the church to see who would provide ultimate values for the young. That night in 1963, the Fox Theater won the opening skirmish.

In taking me to church, my parents were affirming everything that was American. Church was, in a sense, the only show in town. Everybody else was doing it. Church, home and state formed a vast consortium working together to instill Christian values. People grew up Christian, simply by growing up American.

All that ended the night that the Fox Theater opened on Sunday. While my parents or their forebears assumed that the culture would help prop up the church, almost no one believes that today.[5]

Willimon shows the linkage between the mainline Protestant churches and American culture in his statement, "People grew up Christian, simply by growing up American." That has been the point of view of the mainline Protestant denominations since the founding of this country.

But during the second half of this century a significant percentage of the membership of the mainline Protestant denominations saw that to grow up American is not necessarily to grow up Christian, that coherence between the church and American culture no longer exists. In many ways this insight came from the

5. William H. Willimon, "Making Christians in a Secular World," *Christian Century*, 22 October 1986, p. 914.

youth of these denominations who, educated sufficiently in the Christian faith, came to believe that American society was unjust. It began with the Civil Rights Movement. The youth grew impatient with the "establishment" for tolerating injustice. Next, they disagreed with the nation's involvement in Vietnam. On this point they grew angry with their government and society. In the 1960s and early 1970s the youth of this nation were disillusioned, if not angry, and others were beginning to look through their eyes and agree. It wasn't long before serious cleavage developed within the mainline Protestant denominations, within congregations, and within Christian families. Bring to mind the description in the early chapters of this book of the issues that came to divide Christians: civil rights, Vietnam, poverty, hunger, Central America, nuclear armaments, etc. As Stotts puts it, "All these and other concerns became illustrations for many of the mainline Protestant churches' institutional elites, as well as for many pewsitters, that the nation was no longer a carrier of values that could be affirmed by the churches. Even talk of resistance to the government has recently arisen."[6] But an equal number of members, clergy and laity alike, held on to the hope that hurried conclusions about a fracture between the mainline Protestant churches and the state were not warranted, that the historic coherence between church and government could be maintained. This "division of the house" accounts for some of the pain which the mainline Protestant denominations have experienced in recent decades.

But what of the other developments that allegedly are happening, namely, pluralism and secularism? The mainline Protestant denominations know, intellectually at least, *about* pluralism. They hold that there should be a separation of church and state; for example, there should be no reading of the Bible and no prayer offered in the public schools. But the implications of a breakdown in the old coherence has so many far-reaching implications, and the activities to counterbalance these implications are so meager as to be nonexistent, that it is questionable whether

6. Stotts, p. 8.

the full weight of the meaning of pluralism has indeed dawned upon the church.

It is even less clear that the mainline Protestant denominations really sense that contemporary American values are not the church's values. In this respect the mainline Protestant denominations seem to be more objects of secularization than prophets speaking out against it. I have to conclude that the mainline Protestant churches have been initiated into the issue of Christ and culture but that they are far from seeing how much they themselves have been influenced by American society, and even farther from coming to grips with this influence.

To summarize for a moment, while the mainline Protestant denominations historically were very closely aligned with American culture, since World War II that alliance has been fractured. There are four causes of this fracture: differences over policies of the American government; differences over the values pursued in American culture; the new pluralistic landscape in America enabled by the First Amendment; and the loss of transcendence and the subsequent pervasiveness of secularism in American culture.

These factors bring the mainline Protestant denominations to an historic moment. Not all denominations, congregations, and individual Christians are affected in the same way and to the same extent by these changes. Therefore not all of them react in the same way. For example, churches and individual Christians in small towns and rural areas may not feel the full weight of pluralism that churches and Christians in cities feel. Similarly, changing values in American society may affect persons living in small towns and rural areas less than those living in urban areas, though the media is a great leveler. In addition, some Christians "read" the relationship with the American government differently than do other Christians. For some Christians it is difficult to "overthrow in one's soul" the historic position of giving allegiance to the civil authorities. A sense of the orderliness of life is still another factor with which some Christians must contend. Christians have honest differences over the Christ and culture issue. The church is in turmoil over this historic turn of events.

118

THE RESPONSE OF FUNDAMENTALISM

The reaction of some of the fundamentalists to this loss of coherence between the mainline Protestant denominations and the American government has been interesting, to say the least, and it helps to see varying positions in the Christ and culture debate. Some of the fundamentalists have quickly tried to fill the vacuum left by the disaffiliation of the mainline Protestant denominations with the American government. Historically, the fundamentalists have been in the position of being "on the outside looking in." Their traditional position with regard to the Christ and culture debate is that of "Christ against culture"; theirs has historically been an other-worldly position. However, with one born-again American president following another, and with the mainline Protestant denominations abandoning their alignment with the American government, some of the fundamentalists have gladly come to the defense of the policies of the American government—policies which alienated many mainline Protestants—and they have developed a close working relationship with the American presidency. With this possibility open to them, some fundamentalists seemingly have abandoned their other-worldly position. It is also basically the fundamentalists who are pressing for Bible reading and prayer in the public schools, a mixing of religion and politics which historically fundamentalists have opposed.

But quick conclusions should not be drawn. Fundamentalism appears to be in a state of confusion over the Christ and culture issue no less than the mainline Protestant denominations, though fundamentalists may be heading in two different directions, like the proverbial ships passing in the night. Some fundamentalists seem to be flirting with the position of "Christ transforming culture," while others maintain their historic position of "Christ against culture." Let me illustrate.

The authors of a book on an evangelical approach to higher education begin their book—the very first words—as follows: "There were no riots at Wheaton. While students shouted and chanted at Berkeley, burned and looted at Wisconsin, and invaded administration offices all over the country, Wheaton stu-

119

dents went quietly to class, spread out Sundays for ministries in schools and churches in Chicago and the suburbs, and maintained a reassuring calm."[7] This opening statement clearly declares the other-worldly approach of many fundamentalists. The task of the church, according to this traditional fundamentalist point of view, is to minister, not to be engaged in politics or to become too deeply involved in American society. (Incidentally, many members of the mainline Protestant denominations applaud that point of view too.)

A different—and new—point of view for fundamentalism comes from proponents of the electronic gospel—Jim and Tammy Bakker, for example. On the one hand, the fact that the Bakkers operated a Christian amusement park might suggest that they live with one foot in the traditional category of "Christ against culture." On the other hand, their affluence, their mannerisms, their bouts with immorality, and their strong desire to continue a lifestyle more in keeping with Hollywood movie stars than fundamentalist leaders is an indication that they are willing to make considerable accommodations with American culture. Jerry Falwell was lured briefly into the "Christ-transforming-culture" position when he accepted the leadership of the PTL. But more recently Falwell abandoned the PTL *and* the Moral Majority, stating publicly that he was going back to simply preaching the gospel—returning to the traditional fundamentalist position of "Christ against culture." How the fundamentalists will resolve their confusion over Christ and culture is yet to be seen, but it is clear that the seismic changes in American culture have affected fundamentalism as well as the mainline Protestant denominations.

THE CHALLENGE TO THE MAINLINE PROTESTANT DENOMINATIONS

Up to this point, the mainline Protestant denominations have reacted to these seismic changes in a variety of ways ranging from one

7. Marvin K. Mayers, Lawrence O. Richards, Robert Webber, *Reshaping Evangelical Higher Education* (Grand Rapids: Zondervan, 1972), p. 9.

end of the continuum to the other, with some sectors favoring continued alignment with American culture and others calling for a break with American culture. My point of view favors neither extreme. However, the changes in American culture—in government, in society's values, in pluralism, and in secularism—appear so significant that the status quo is unacceptable. The mainline Protestant denominations must make discussion of Christ and culture a top priority. This discussion is mandatory. Doing nothing, as if nothing had changed, is unacceptable. If the changes in American culture which I have just summarized are in fact occurring, then inactivity on the part of the mainline Protestant denominations will lead to what Jack Stotts called "the banality of the church."[8]

Willimon points the mainline Protestant churches in a new direction. He elevates the synagogue as a model and suggests that we have come to a time when the church must consider itself a "peculiar people" in American culture. He cites a Jewish rabbi who said to him: "We are forever telling our young, 'That's fine for everyone else, but it's not fine for you. You are special. You are different. You are a Jew. We have different values, a different story.'"[9] Willimon observes, "I believe that the day is coming, has already come, when the church must again take seriously the task of making Christians—of intentionally forming a peculiar people."[10]

Willimon goes on to say that in this new situation, churches must change their approach to church life, that instead of relying almost solely on the image of "nurture," the church must think more in terms of "conversion." When the culture was Christian, the image of nurture was all right. In this new situation, the culture is not Christian and therefore the church must begin from a different point of view. Willimon says that once again the church must begin, as the Reformers did, with an "externum verbum," an external word. Willimon writes:

8. Jack L. Stotts, "The Banality of Religion" (Paper given at the sesquicentennial celebration of Muskingum College, New Concord, Ohio, 1987, mimeo.), p. 1.

9. Willimon, "Making Christians," p. 914.

10. *Ibid.*, p. 915.

> So the first task of the church is *formation* rather than *education*—
> not to bring out, but to bring to. The task of Christian educators
> is not to develop an individual's potential. . . , but rather to induct
> us into the faith community, to give us the skills, insights, words,
> stories and rituals that we need to live this faith in a world that
> neither knows nor follows the One who is truth. . . . Formation
> implies the existence of an intentional, visible community made
> up of people who are willing to pay the price of community . . . to
> be the Body of Christ in which members assume responsibility for
> one another's faith and morals. . . .What is needed is an honest
> admission of our changed status. . . .The church must now com-
> pete, in an open market, with other claimants for the truth.[11]

A key concept in Willimon as to how the church must live
and function in this new environment is *community*. The church
is made up of a group of interdependent persons who care for
each other, a group of persons who are related to one another because they are the Body of Christ. One of their functions *as a community* is to guide, direct, and support one another in their faith.

What does all of the above discussion suggest for the mainline Protestant denominations? First, we must recognize that the
American culture about which we are speaking is new. Therefore, some caution is due lest we overreact—a uniquely American response.

But surely Willimon is right in pointing out that pluralism
alone has changed the *context* in which the mainline Protestant
denominations find themselves. These denominations must give
serious attention to the implications of this pluralism. It may very
well call for a considerably different starting point for the church.
The way in which Jews have had to live in various cultures
throughout history may provide the church with a helpful model.
Surely parents who take their Christian faith seriously must, like
Willimon's rabbi friend, point out to their children that they are
different, that their values and goals are to be different than those
held by their neighbors. And surely this pluralism has profound
implications for the educational programs of the mainline Prot-

11. *Ibid.*, pp. 915-17.

estant churches. Churches and families cannot ask American culture to nurture their children and youth in the Christian faith. Yet on how many denominations, congregations, and families has this fully dawned? And when will it be realized fully enough that it will be pursued with seriousness? The issue of "formation" that Willimon raises is a critical one which needs immediate attention. Just how will Christians be formed in a pluralistic society?

These denominations, congregations, and families must also pursue the implications of secularism as well as the policies of the American government and the values by which many Americans are living. This is an area where more consideration must be given to just which approach to culture will be most effective. Granted, there will be no "quick fix," perhaps no real solutions at all, for these areas. At the same time, I do not believe that the mainline Protestant denominations should too quickly call themselves aliens in American culture and separate from it.

The mainline Protestant denominations must consider carefully whether it is better or more appropriate to work toward influencing American culture from a distance or from within. The church may need to live with ambiguity and frustration while it attempts to influence and enrich American culture. There is a spectrum on which the church must place itself with regard to American culture. Honest Christians will differ on just where the church should be on this spectrum. On the one hand, the church can no longer identify itself synonymously with American culture. On the other hand, the church should not automatically write off American culture either. The church must be more thoughtful, intentional, and discerning than it has had to be in the past. In this respect, the church's life will be more difficult in the future than it has been in the past.

Stotts suggests that already the mainline Protestant denominations have become frustrated over their decreased leverage with the policies of the American government now that they have distanced themselves from the government.[12] The church may need to live with a considerable amount of ambiguity and frustra-

12. Stotts, "The Seismic Shift," p. 10.

tion and attempt to maintain its historic tie to the American government as an alternative to developing distance. This topic needs a great deal of further discussion in the church.

But lest all of the attention on this subject be focused outwardly on American culture, the agenda of the mainline Protestant denominations is to be free from the pervasive influence of secularism. The church must give immediate and thorough attention to its most basic confession, "Jesus Christ is Lord," and to the meaning of that confession for the church living in American culture. The church needs to give attention to theology and worship in addition to ethics. The church needs to rediscover its transcendent source of life and its identity.

CHURCH-RELATED COLLEGES AND AMERICAN CULTURE

We come now to the tough question about the relationship between the church-related college and contemporary American culture.

As we outlined in earlier chapters, many of these colleges have fallen under the influence of the secular university. They have been influenced by the so-called value-free approach, basically a secular approach to education. Most have been influenced by the Cartesian-Newtonian paradigm and have allowed religion to become merely a subject for study alongside the other academic disciplines, instead of the integrating factor it once was and ought to be. Under these conditions, many of these colleges may not wish to accept our changed position or to do anything about it. One wonders how those church-related colleges which are so thoroughly secular will be able to critique American culture. How will they gain a perspective? On what basis will they critique secularism?

The first order of business for the church-related colleges is to reacquaint themselves with the major Christian tenets. They should regain their spiritual heritage and their theological foundation. Second, they must get themselves out from under the Cartesian-Newtonian paradigm and reshape their lives on the basis of the post-modern science paradigm of integration and wholeness. Only then will they be equipped to tackle the issue of Christ and culture that we face in the wake of the seismic shift in American culture.

The mission of the college is not the same as that of the church. The mission of the college is not conversion, though there may be events on the campus which promote conversion. The mission of the college is education. However, that educational point of view should be so designed and constructed that the major tenets of the Christian faith are clear. The entire educational enterprise of the church-related college should be Christocentric. The church-related college should point out a clear, Christian alternative to the secular viewpoint of the public university and American culture. In light of the seismic shift that has taken place, the church-related college cannot rely upon American culture any more than the church can to carry out its educational mission. The college must be very intentional in shaping its educational program. In addition, its faculty and administration should be recruited in such a way that they work in concert with the program to present students with a clear, if diverse, Christian viewpoint. The church-related college is a great place to discuss Christ and culture when the school is so grounded in the Christian faith that it can critique American culture and show how the Christian faith calls people to be different. The church-related college ought to prepare its graduates to take their place in American culture and to bring to it a Christian perspective.

A great deal has happened in higher education since the Second World War, much of it sad. Currently we are in a shakedown period in higher education. This is a great time, therefore, for the church and the church-related college—as partners—to build a new *raison d'être* for the church-related college, one that will enrich the church, redirect the college, and influence American society.

If the church-related college fulfills this mission, then it can also be of inestimable assistance to the church as it attempts to develop its response to the new challenge of the relationship between Christ and culture. The church-related college is a very good place for some of the thinking that the church must do. It can be a part of the church's "community" as the church thinks and contemplates. It can be a source of points of view to help the church think about policies of the government. Isolated as many of these colleges are from the busyness of everyday life, these campuses can provide the necessary quiet time for the church to reflect. The mix of students and faculty provides an opportunity for the church to dream and have visions of how things might be in the future. These campuses are full of idealism which can both lead and invigorate the church. These colleges can be places where lively discussion is held about the meaning of the Lordship of Christ and what shape and form that Lordship will take in the future in American society and in our world.

If these church-related colleges will form their identity and establish their *raison d'être* around the major Christian tenets, they can be of inestimable help first to their students but also to the church, and thus to American culture.

III. Application of New Principles

8. New Direction for the Church-Related College

We have traced the changes in American society, in the mainline Protestant denominations, and in higher education since the Second World War. We have described the diminished impact of the Christian faith upon higher education. We have observed the effect which the "modern science paradigm" has had upon higher education. We have seen the changed position of Protestantism vis-à-vis American culture. We have laid the theoretical foundation for a new *raison d'être* for the church-related college based upon the major tenets of the Christian faith and the "post-modern science paradigm" within a pluralistic society. The time has now come to apply these new principles in this new context to the church-related college. That is the purpose of this final section of the book.

New directions for church-related colleges will be best found if this book is used as a study and discussion book and if many others take up the invitation to seek out, describe, and extend the implications set forth here. I encourage group discussions within church-related colleges and within churches, using this book as a stimulus. It should be understood from the outset therefore that what this section of the book does is make a beginning at listing the many applications of these principles.

Church-related colleges must have a clear understanding of their nature and mission. If the church is to continue to support these colleges and if the American public is to continue to support these colleges through tuition and private gifts, these colleges must shape their educational enterprises very consciously and purposely, and they must clearly articulate their nature and mission to the church and to the public. Much more so than they have done in the past three or four decades, the church-related colleges must define who they are, what they stand for, and what it is they are trying to accomplish with their students. The nature and mission of these colleges should be based upon the major Christian tenets and the post-modern science paradigm, with the realization that the Christian faith—its institutions and adherents—must function in a pluralistic environment with diverse religions, value systems, and philosophies, and that the prevailing point of view in American culture is secular, not Christian. To present a clear, Christian point of view within higher education in this changed environment is the challenge which the church-related colleges face.

Approximately every decade, each college ought to engage in a planning process which begins with the creation of a statement of its nature and mission. A broad range of persons representing all of the constituencies of the college—trustees, students, alumni, faculty members, administrators, and members of the local community—ought to discuss the nature and mission of the college. After broad discussion, a mission statement should be drafted and should receive final approval by the faculty and the board of trustees. Based upon this mission statement, further planning should then shape the total educational enterprise of the college to fit this mission statement. Study groups made up of appropriate persons should look at all sectors of the college and shape the life and development of the college according to the mission statement. Such planning, when done in this collegial fashion, incorporates new ideas and generates commitment to the overall mission of the college. Having such broadly based involvement helps to insure that the college will treat the mission statement as a lively, critically important instrument.

The board of trustees must play a more vital role in creating and overseeing this mission statement than has been customary in the past. Sometimes the trustees treat this process as an obligatory one, peculiar to academe, a process to which they must pay homage. More often they leave this process to the administration and faculty with little interest in whether or not it is taken seriously. Such an attitude signals to the rest of the academic community that the overall direction of the college can be taken for granted or is of little importance. The trustees must treat with all seriousness the process of shaping and living by a mission statement. The trustees set the tone. If they are serious about the nature and mission of the college, there is a much better chance that the rest of the college will take this process seriously; the result will be a college with an appropriate and clearly stated mission statement that guides its entire life.

The trustees should also assure that the subsequent planning groups carry out their assignments so that all dimensions of the college function within the larger mission statement and promote and enhance its goals. If church-related colleges are to meet the challenge of a meaningful *raison d'être,* it will be, in large part, because the trustees demanded an appropriate and clearly stated mission statement and because they made sure that the college vigorously pursued the goals articulated in that statement.

If one important task of the board of trustees is to oversee the creation and implementation of the mission statement, another important task is the selection of a president who believes in, personifies, and promotes the nature and mission of the college. The first task of the president after coordinating the creation or clarification of the college's mission statement is to ensure that all areas of the college seek to fulfill it. In the past, colleges often assumed that all persons at the college generally understood its nature and mission and that all sectors of the college were generally working toward shared mission goals. This assumption and style have proved unacceptable. It has often led church-related colleges to be indistinguishable from the secular universities except in size and cost.

Our times call for clear alternatives in a pluralistic society. It must be the task of the president to see that the college carries out a planning process, the result of which is a distinct statement of mission, and that all sectors of the college play their part in fulfilling the college's mission. Furthermore, the president must articulate this mission to all constituencies of the college and to the general public. The president is in the pivotal position internally and externally with regard to the mission of the college. This is one of the most important tasks of the president to which the trustees must hold him accountable.

Just as the president is critical in shaping and implementing the mission statement, so are the cabinet officers who work directly under the president. The president should select cabinet members with great care since all of the other persons working at the college are selected by and work under the cabinet officers. The cabinet officers, like the president, should be excited about and committed to the distinct mission of their college. They should grasp how the mission statement affects the various sectors of the college, including their own, and how these sectors complement one another under the mission statement. They must plan and supervise their own sector in such a way that it promotes and fulfills the mission statement. Like the president, the cabinet officers should personify the mission both inside and outside the college, since they have many opportunities to relate to the general public.

The faculty at a church-related college should be selected with special care. The dean of the college should give critical attention to the task of recruitment so that only persons who share enthusiastically the aims and purposes of the college are brought there. A college is a marketplace for ideas, values, worldviews, and belief systems. More than any other group, the faculty interact with students in this marketplace. Rather than being "value free," faculty members should be "value laden." Their ideas, value systems, worldviews, and belief systems should be present on the campus for the students to see and consider. This is the *raison d'être* of the church-related college. Faculty recruitment, carried out by the dean of the college, under the supervision of the president, is one of the most significant tasks in shaping and insuring the nature and mission of a church-related college. Time, effort, and money must be devoted to this critical task.

Other administrators and staff members—including secretaries, custodians, cooks, maintenance, and grounds personnel— also play an important role in embodying and articulating the nature and mission of the college. Nonfaculty personnel, simply because they are not involved in the pressured teacher-student relationship, often grow very close to students and can be helpful to students at critical times. These persons, through example and words, are an integral part of the community which surrounds, supports, and directs students.

It is important that enough persons who believe in, exemplify, and articulate ideas, values, worldviews, and belief systems consistent with the college's viewpoint be present on the campus as the students shape their lives. Few tasks are as important as the selection of this total community of persons. After establishing the nature and mission of a church-related college, the next most important task is the recruitment of college personnel who believe in and who promote that mission.

In an earlier chapter we discussed two legitimate approaches to Christian higher education: focusing only on the "intellectual virtues," as Aristotle called them, or focusing on both the "intellectual virtues" *and* the "moral virtues." The context in which we live—a secular and pluralistic society—more than ever calls the church-related college to emphasize *both* the intellectual and the moral virtues. In language with which we are perhaps more familiar, this means focusing on both faith and learning. However, more than merely focusing on faith and learning— for this can mean pursuing faith and learning side by side—the church-related college must focus on the *integration* of faith and learning. Church-related colleges must take this further step. Students must not simply be offered faith and learning in separate and unrelated packages, so to speak, but students should observe how faith gives direction and meaning to learning and see how learning enriches and enlarges faith.

Sometimes this issue is played out in the way a given college perceives its "relationship" with its sponsoring denomination. Some colleges identify themselves with a particular denomination. They offer religion courses through a department of religion. They may also have a campus minister and hold worship services on campus or through a nearby church. The end result, by design or by chance, is that, while there is both faith *and* learning, the two seldom meet or co-mingle. The denominations have been able to replicate such an approach to faith and learning in their university campus ministries.

Our times call for a more dynamic encounter, a closer relationship between faith and learning. Church-related colleges should go beyond this type of parallel relationship to the point where the entire college community and the total educational enterprise seek to *integrate* faith and learning. Such integration is in keeping with the Christian tenets and the post-modern science paradigm, which call for integration, connectedness, and wholeness.

It is at this point that many church-related colleges must rethink their nature and mission and the implications of what it means to be a church-related college. I encourage the colleges affiliated with the mainline Protestant denominations not only to pursue the intellectual and moral virtues—to pursue faith and learning—but to *integrate* the intellectual and moral virtues, to *integrate* faith and learning. The parallel relationship is the product of the Cartesian-Newtonian paradigm. It is inadequate; it is erroneous. Church-related colleges should abandon this old paradigm in favor of shaping their educational enterprise on the Christian tenets and the post-modern science paradigm, and thereby pursue integration and wholeness.

In urging the integration of faith and learning, I know that I am in sensitive territory. Old images come to mind of the way faith attempted to control or even diminish learning. But the pendulum has swung too far in the opposite direction to a point where learning has become totally secular, where learning is captive to a secular point of view. What I am calling for in urging the integration of faith and learning is a free and equal partnership. There must be Christian freedom at the church-related college. Everything is open to inquiry. There should be as much opportunity to doubt and question as to believe. There must also be as much opportunity to believe as there is to doubt and question.

The purpose of calling for the integration of faith and learning is not to mold either faith or learning in one fashion or another but to assist the student in putting together an integrated life during the formative college years. Such an integrated life calls for the enrichment of faith and learning, but more than that it calls for the integration of these two dimensions *within the student.* The beauty of a church-related college is that such integration, mutual enrichment, and enlargement can go on. We are seeing spiritual bankruptcy in individuals, in our civic leadership, and generally in a society where faith has not been integrated with learning. We are also seeing in the life of the church the effects of the loss of the intellectual and cultural dimensions. Learning needs faith and faith needs learning—within the student, within the church, and within our society. This is the challenge which the church-related colleges have before them.

Perhaps describing how such integration is accomplished in the church-related college may help to alleviate some fears. We must begin by changing the focus from the curriculum to the student. In the minds of many people, particularly in this age of information and specialization, the curriculum has become the major focus. From this perspective, the task of faculty members is to impart information and skills to students, not values.

Contrary to such thinking, I believe that *the student* must be the focus of attention—the student's total growth. When the student's total growth is the focus of the educational enterprise, some of the issues change. The issue is not whether there is such a thing as Christian mathematics or chemistry, but whether all faculty members—whatever their academic discipline—use and offer all of themselves as they work to enrich and enlarge their students. The integration of faith and learning takes place in the classroom some of the time and outside the classroom some of the time. It takes place as people interact with people, when students listen to lectures and observe faculty members function in their profession, when students argue with faculty members, and when they are counseled by faculty members. What is true of faculty members can be said of administrators and other staff members as well. Faculty members at church-related colleges ought not to hide behind their specialties; they cannot fulfill their obligation to students by simply imparting information and developing skills, but rather by interacting *as total persons* with the total person of the student. Faculty members at church-related colleges are their brother's (and sister's) keeper in the classroom and beyond. The focus at a church-related college is not on what the faculty members have, but upon who they are and upon who the students are becoming. Again, both the Christian faith and the post-modern science paradigm call for the integration of the faculty member. Through the faculty member's own integration will come the integration and growth of faith and learning in the student.

If the goal of the church-related college is the development of the whole student—as it should be according to the major Christian tenets and the post-modern science paradigm—then the organization of the college should reflect this goal. After the Second World War and under the influence of the Cartesian-Newtonian paradigm, colleges separated the intellectual growth of their students from the students' social growth. Colleges appointed an academic dean to lead the faculty toward the intellectual growth of the student and appointed a dean of students and additional staff members to look after the social dimensions of the student. It should also be noted that, with a few exceptions, most colleges paid much closer attention to the intellectual growth of the student than to the student's social growth. Even when colleges did pay attention to the whole student, it was often done in a piecemeal and halfhearted way.

I suggest that church-related colleges pay considerably more attention to the total growth of the student—intellectual, social, spiritual, even physical—and that the organization of the colleges reflect this focus on the total person of the student. One way to reflect this goal organizationally would be to have a dean of the "learning program," the learning program being comprised of what are now the academic and student-life areas. I encourage the faculty to be much more involved in shaping, critiquing, and encouraging all features of the learning program so that the total development of the student is the major goal of the college. The administration and faculty should work in a cooperative, integrated way to develop, implement, critique, and improve the total learning program of the college. Such an approach will best match what is suggested by the Christian tenets and the postmodern science paradigm.

Historically there has been a close tie between the Christian faith and liberal-arts education. This tie should continue. The aim of a liberal education is to have faculty member and student together ask and attempt to answer the major human questions, to seek to establish the alternative answers, values, and philosophies of life. Perhaps more basic than this, a liberal-arts education establishes in the student's mind the fact that there are alternative routes in life, that the human is a thinking, reflecting, and deciding being, that life is there for the shaping. It is called "liberal" education because it frees humans from the confines of instinct and enriches man's sense that he is a being of choices, that he can change himself and his environment, that life can be different than it has been, that it is opportunity. It is in this sense that a liberal-arts education helps man exercise his God-given nature as a thinking and acting being. The tie between the Christian faith and a liberal-arts education is a profoundly theological one.

Furthermore, the subject matter and the accompanying skills of a liberal-arts education deal with the basic core knowledge and skills of human knowing. A liberal-arts education is the prerequisite knowledge of all human learning. The church should promote the widest possible participation in the development of the human being. In addition, because it is precisely in the issues pursued in a liberal arts and sciences curriculum that the basic questions and issues of human existence are pursued, a liberal-arts education is the major marketplace of ideas and values in our society. The church must be a part of liberal-arts education in order to present the Christian viewpoint in this marketplace.

I have pointed out the importance of a liberal-arts education, and earlier I indicated that the church-related college should attempt to develop the whole of the student. Let me share two metaphors which may help in the pursuit of such a holistic approach to education at the church-related college.

The first metaphor is "growing oak trees." One of the trustees of Muskingum College, Mr. Philip Caldwell, who was the CEO of Ford Motor Company, described the kind of person he looked for in the top executive personnel of his company. "We like to have whole people, not sunflowers. Consider the shape of the sunflower plant. As it grows, it has a stalk that is tall and thin and no branches. When the head comes on the seeds develop. It has a very big head and then at some stage the head drops. We'd rather have oak trees with many branches and strengths so that when you get to the top there is a lot to draw on. . . . We would like to see people in different disciplines, in different geographical areas, dealing with assignments that have different priorities. We want to grow whole people, not sunflowers."[1]

Growing oak trees is a helpful metaphor for the liberal-arts, church-related college which wishes to develop the whole of the student. Think of the student as an oak tree to be nurtured to maturity. The trunk is developed through the general education curriculum and through elements of the student development program, which together pursue the intellectual, social, spiritual, and physical growth of the student. Such a program, which is rooted in the unique heritage and identity of a given college and which includes in the learning program the richness of our cultural heritage along with the basic communication and analytic skills, shapes the student into a firm, resourceful, and knowledgeable person. From this deep rootage, this strong trunk, and these sturdy limbs, the student is able to grow a rich combination of branches and leaves. Attempting to shape students as oak trees results in persons of vitality and strength, symmetry, resourcefulness, and longevity. The church-related college, with its interest in pursuing both faith and learning, may be aided in thinking of the educational process as growing oak trees.

An alternative use of this metaphor is to view the learning

1. Philip Caldwell, "This I Believe," *Lessons in Success and Leadership,* Nightingale-Conant Corporation, tape recording.

program as an oak tree, though, as I said earlier, the student, not the learning program, should be the focus of attention. The church-related college may wish to view its total learning program as an oak tree. Rootage comes from the college's intellectual and spiritual heritage, providing the college with its basic ethos. The general education program is the trunk and major limbs of the oak tree. From the roots, trunk, and major limbs grow the branches and leaves. The total picture is one of vitality, strength, resourcefulness, longevity, symmetry, uniqueness, and beauty. Note that if any one of the human dimensions is left out— intellectual, social, spiritual, or physical—the tree suffers and is diminished. It is in designing the total learning program of the college, with all dimensions of the student's life in mind, that the church-related college fulfills its challenge of educating the whole student.

A second metaphor is "opening roads." Muskingum College, located on U.S. Highway 40 (sometimes called the National Road), celebrated its sesquicentennial anniversary with the theme "opening roads" because it was founded when the National Road was laid from the East Coast, over the Appalachian Mountains, and onto the plains. This theme proved to be a helpful metaphor. "Opening roads" suggests the obligation which a liberal-arts, church-related college has to open each student to the opportunities which they individually have in a liberal arts education. It also can be a metaphor for each student who takes advantage of the many growth opportunities at a college which takes the total growth of the student seriously.

At Muskingum College the metaphor was understood as follows. Just as the early citizens—great and small—of this young country, through a lofty vision, through courageous planning, and through blood, sweat, and tears, cut out and established a road that brought untold opportunity to the citizens of this nation, so the early frontier people, also through a lofty vision, and with blood, sweat, and tears, courageously fought against great obstacles, established, and for 150 years maintained this college. Our forebears opened roads: that is, they provided inestimable opportunities for thousands of students to be educated. The educational process itself is a process of opening roads, of opening vistas and opportunities for students.

The metaphor "opening roads" describes the process of a liberal-arts education. The heritage and ethos of the college are available, as are the faculty members with their knowledge, values, and skills, to open students to vision and growth. A more detailed description of catching a vision and becoming open to growth can help a church-related, liberal-arts college plan its program. Most students who attend college bring some goals with them. Parents, teachers, and other mentors helped to instill in the students the desire for growth. They arrive at college wanting to grow.

What is it that opens within students while they are in college? First, students develop a vision of who they might be as adults. Their horizons are expanded; they are ready to grasp a larger world. Their perception becomes greater; they connect themselves with more and different people, with different points of view, issues, and causes. They gather more knowledge and sharpen the skills which accompany this knowledge in order to handle their expanding world, but also to find a vocational niche in adult society. They open themselves to and make more connections with the past as they prepare for the future, all of which makes their present dynamic, expanding, and filled with possibilities. The entire milieu and ethos of the college—people, books, laboratories, plays, work, concerts, athletic contests, buzz sessions in the dormitory, etc.—are each a part of this opening process. The college works hard and purposefully to insure the richness, breadth, and vitality of this opening process.

There is a kind of progression to this opening process. Early on there must be a vision of what the student might become as well as a vision of what kind of world the student wants to live in. Throughout the college experience there is the ongoing acquisition of knowledge and the sharpening of skills. That knowledge and these skills are constructed on a larger "grid of life" which the student's vision has helped to create. Students become acquainted with the past—including values, theories, events, and information—and learn to analyze, criticize, sort out, accept, discard, and thus reach decisions. They move closer to adult citizens as they begin to visualize their niche in society. Sensing this niche, they begin to think about how they will function in society as adults. Not only do they begin to picture themselves functioning in that society, but they develop an idealized picture of what the world might become in the future.

As students move through their last two years of college, they gain a larger, more balanced perspective; they develop increasing resourcefulness and judgment, and there is an increasing eagerness to get out into the adult world. Self-esteem and self-confidence increase. With the help of internships or extra-curricular activities, students learn how to put knowledge and skills into action. They often strive for positions of leadership on campus, partly for the boost in self-esteem and growth in self-confidence which such activities bring, but also to try out and develop their leadership skills. With some initial success in leadership, students develop within themselves a greater sense of responsibility not only for themselves but for their organizations as well, and gradually also for their society. By graduation, they have a sense of satisfaction, considerable growth in self-confidence, and an eagerness to enter the full adult world.

The total college experience is a process of putting knowledge and skills into the context of a value system, articulating that knowledge, those skills, and that value system into the students' visions of themselves and their world. The result is a fulfilling life, one in which continued openness and enlargement are enjoyed throughout life. That is what the metaphor "opening roads" suggests.

It should be obvious how important a holistic approach to a liberal-arts education is when viewed through this metaphor, how important it is for faculty members and administrators to merge the academic and student development programs into one integrated, carefully designed and implemented learning program. It is also easy to see how important it is to help the student develop the moral and spiritual dimensions of life at the same time that the intellectual, social, and physical dimensions are being nurtured. The result of such a holistic goal and such an integrated learning program is a whole student.

Under the influence of the Cartesian-Newtonian paradigm, the curriculum at most, if not all, church-related colleges has been organized around the separate academic disciplines and departments. Even most, if not all, of the general education courses are selected from a list of courses from each academic department rather than being organized together as courses in their own right—although there has been a movement in that direction in the past decade. While in recent years a few integrated courses have been offered, the majority of the curriculum remains organized around the separate academic disciplines. It has been left to the students somehow to integrate the knowledge and skills they have gained from these separate disciplines.

The Christian tenets and the post-modern science paradigm call for the integration of knowledge. Church-related colleges should seek ways to offer students a more integrated curriculum to match the wholeness which they are attempting to develop in students. In most colleges the way in which the curriculum is organized contradicts the mission of the college to develop whole persons. The curriculum at a church-related college should demonstrate the connectedness of knowledge, the connectedness of reality.

This is a tough challenge for faculties to meet because faculty members are themselves the products of such separated curricula; they have been functioning as specialists within separated disciplines and are uncomfortable, even threatened, if they are called upon to cross disciplinary boundaries. Furthermore, general inertia in academe makes such a massive change difficult. It is also a tough challenge because no new method of integrating the curriculum has been offered, at least not one that has been attractive enough to draw faculties from the separated approach to an integrated approach. Also mitigating against change is our society's call for specialists, though more voices are beginning to be heard calling for more broadly educated graduates.

Before sketching an integrated approach, let me make what will surely be perceived by many as a heretical suggestion. I suggest that we place less emphasis in the liberal arts college on the major. The major—at least as it is currently designed—is a product of the Cartesian-Newtonian paradigm. I suggest that a student be given the *option* whether or not he wishes to have a major. If the student chooses not to have a major, the rules of the college ought to require the student to take a balanced number of courses throughout the liberal arts and sciences curricula, balanced between lower- and upper-level courses. Currently, college faculties explicitly and self-assuredly require a major. I cannot remember the last time I have heard a discussion on this topic. It has been assumed without an explicit rationale that having a major is a virtue. I believe that some students, perhaps many students, would receive a better, more balanced liberal arts education if they had to participate more broadly and in greater depth in the total liberal arts and sciences curriculum. And the more integration there is among curricula, the more valuable for students. The major has become a shibboleth that needs evaluation in the light of the post-modern science paradigm.

Turning now to a suggestion of how a church-related, liberal-arts college's curriculum might be organized in an integrated fashion, I would approach the curriculum in an historical fashion, focusing largely but not exclusively upon the history of Western civilization. The unique values and religious point of view of a given college can be woven into the fabric of such an historical approach, thus giving the college a means of pursuing its unique mission. I would break up history into meaningful eras which would be pursued a semester at a time. Building on such an historical grid, the religions, values, political philosophies and institutions, social structures, art, architecture, music, literature, language, and drama would be discussed. Students would see the progression of our civilization and they would see how all dimensions of knowledge, indeed of civilization, are interconnected. Professor Milton Reigelman at Centre College describes the beauty and meaning of teaching when the academic disciplines are integrated:

> To begin to see the Parthenon as a unifying symbol of Greek art, mathematics, philosophy, and drama is to begin to glimpse Emerson's unity in diversity. To study the *Divine Comedy* and

Chartres at the same time is to make a discovery about the brilliant coherence of the medieval mind and therefore possibly our own. Literature scholars everywhere have taught *Pride and Prejudice,* many with great success. But to teach it in a course that also considers another comprehensive 18th-century structure—Mozart's Symphony No. 40—coaxes you out of your scholarly pigeonhole into a wider, richer world, and causes you to read and teach your "own" literature—in my case, 19th- and 20th-century American novels—with a new understanding of the subtle ways motifs and moods determine meaning.[2]

With such a solid base of knowledge, and with the connectedness made obvious to them, students could select one area to pursue in depth if a major is required. But even the courses in the major could more easily be integrated by faculty members and students alike, as Professor Reigelman suggests, if the major was built on such a solid, broad, and integrated curriculum.

I offer this as a suggestion. While I am serious in this suggestion, it is also given to stimulate other persons to work at this process of designing and experimenting with an integrated curriculum. We need creative suggestions from a variety of sources in order to break away from the old approach and to be compelled by a new, integrated approach to the liberal arts and sciences curriculum.

Let me briefly cite a few additional ways in which integration, connectedness, and wholeness should affect the learning program, with the hope that these will stimulate other persons to add to this list.

Just as the post-modern science paradigm helps us to see how we are connected to the past, present, and future in a much more dynamic way than we have previously understood, and just as it shows how connected the human is to the rest of the physical universe, so it also shows how connected one human being is to another, without regard to economic status, race, ethnic back-

---

2. Milton Reigelman, "Today's Scholar: 'A Good Finger, A Good Neck, An Elbow, but Never A Man,'" *The Chronicle of Higher Education,* 2 September 1987, p. A128.

ground, political philosophy, or geographical boundaries. The Christian tenets suggest the same connectedness in all of human life. From the first millisecond of Creation, because the velocity was just right, all things were created in dynamic interconnectedness. From the first, God's intention was that of interdependence and interrelatedness. Or take St. Paul's vision of the Christian community, where "there is neither Jew nor Greek, slave nor free, male nor female, for you are all one in Christ Jesus" (Gal. 3:28). I offer two emphases which the church-related college should make as it plays out this connectedness. Church-related colleges should have a strong international emphasis, and they ought to work hard at including minorities and persons of all economic levels. A church-related college cannot pay homage to the Christian tenets and the post-modern science paradigm and not work hard at connectedness and inclusiveness.

One additional dimension to the college's learning program is affected by the concept of connectedness. I believe that church-related colleges ought to give serious consideration to the ways in which their students provide service to their society, and develop viable alternatives. Particularly in a society as steeped in individualism as is contemporary American society, if colleges become too sheltered, too disconnected from society, they will fail to demonstrate and therefore to impress upon each student his or her connectedness to society. Each student is indebted to his or her society, and as he or she reaches maturity, each is responsible for society. This is an important concept almost totally lacking in the current learning programs of our colleges. And if the colleges could tie into a program of universal service which might be developed in this country, so much the better. Church-related colleges in particular should pursue within their learning programs this dimension of human connectedness.

While the Cartesian-Newtonian paradigm suggests that the universe is a closed system, capable of being known, understood, and controlled, the post-modern science paradigm suggests that the universe is open, still in the process of developing, and filled with mystery. These two different viewpoints have pedagogical implications. Instead of the large

145

amounts of ingestion and regurgitation which typify the pedagogy related to the Cartesian-Newtonian paradigm, the postmodern science paradigm suggests that we attempt to create open, searching, and creative minds so that students can participate dynamically within a universe that is still in a state of becoming. The Cartesian-Newtonian paradigm encouraged specialization through a narrow focus; it tended to lead away from education to training. The post-modern science paradigm would have us be more creative, more reflective; it would lead us to plumb things in greater depth and soar to greater heights. Church-related colleges ought to form their educational goals and adopt pedagogical techniques that encourage such openness, reflection, creativity, and imagination.

Let me next address the topic of excellence. *Excellence* is a shibboleth currently very popular in talk about higher education. It is too often used in much the same way that the mass media and advertising use an image or a word, in the belief that if the word is used frequently, the public will believe that excellence is indeed present. Instead of playing this media and advertising game—a game played very well during political campaigns—church-related colleges must in fact shape and implement an excellent learning program which will make a profound and lasting impression upon each of their students.

Excellence at a church-related college means a carefully thought-out mission statement, the goal of which is the growth of the whole person—intellectual, social, spiritual, and physical.

Excellence at a church-related college means carefully selected faculty members and administrators who share in and are enthusiastic about the college's mission, living and working with students, and helping those students move toward a rich maturity.

Excellence at a church-related college means having faculty members, administrators, and other staff members surround the students with a caring attitude, spending time with the students, sharing their own ideas, personalities, values, and faith, always encouraging those students, making demands upon them, complimenting them, cajoling them, but always loving them.

146

Excellence at a church-related college means good teaching, teaching that draws students out, turns them on to learning, encourages them to be creative, imaginative, and independent in their thinking, sharp in their analysis, and positive in their endeavors.

Excellence at a church-related college means shaping a learning program that is consistent with the mission statement of the college—a learning program that does not merely attempt to be traditional for tradition's sake, nor that chases every academic fad, nor that simply insures the college's survival. Excellence calls for a carefully thought-out curriculum with direction, meaning, and dignity.

Excellence at a church-related college calls for a good library, well-equipped laboratories, and other tools to complement the faculty and the curriculum.

Excellence at a church-related college means that the total life of the college is consistent with the mission of the college. It means creating a climate where people work hard at their common tasks as well as play hard in respite from those tasks.

Excellence at a church-related college means looking beyond the campus to the community, to society, and to our world, and giving thought, time, and attention to life beyond the campus, even as a student.

Excellence means having the requisite buildings, grounds, and other facilities whereby an attractive, wholesome environment encourages the daily activities of the academic community.

Excellence means providing students with a wide range of activities—extracurricular and intramural activities, clubs and other organizations, as well as service projects—through which students can be creative, develop commitments, practice leadership skills, and develop self-esteem.

Excellence means not only teaching but also research activities, writing and presenting papers, publishing articles and books, giving concerts and lectures, and creating works of art.

Excellence means engaging in self-criticism, but more than that it means all members of the community taking responsibility for the institution and carrying out a commitment to strengthen it, taking pride in its accomplishments as well as enjoying daily life within its fellowship.

Excellence means the acquisition of important knowledge along with the accompanying skills; but as much—or more—it means learning how to learn, developing the desire to continue to learn, to be curious, to develop and use one's imagination, and to satisfy a creative mind. And it means offering all of this through one's person to others with whom life is shared.

The church-related college should pursue excellence for many reasons. Let me cite just one. In our secular, pluralistic society, the Christian faith is just one alternative, and it no longer holds a favored position. Church-related colleges must shape their learning program into the best possible program, and they must develop their students with the utmost vigor so that an educational program which integrates faith and learning will stand out in our society as the best educational process. It must also be the best to insure that the graduates of the church-related colleges rise to positions of leadership in our society and in our world. It must be the best so that a diversity of domestic as well as international students seek out the church-related college because of its reputation for excellence.

If there are implications of the Christian tenets and the postmodern science paradigm for the learning program, there are also implications for the administration of the college and for the college community as a whole.

The Cartesian-Newtonian paradigm led to division and specialization in college administration just as it did in the academic disciplines. As a result, college administration has become fragmented, impersonal, and bureaucratic. While the church-related college may not be able to rid itself of this specialized type of organization and administration completely (in part because it must respond to external constituencies), it should seek to minimize, if not eliminate, the negative fallout from the Cartesian-Newtonian paradigm. As much as possible, church-related colleges should attempt to organize and administer the college, and all community members should attempt to function within the college, on the basis of the principles of integration, connected-ness, and wholeness.

Every member of the church-related college community should be treated as a whole person, having dignity and worth, and should not be "managed." Management methods and tools, while having value, should not get in the way of the collegial administration of the college. One-to-one communication be-tween persons in the academic community is essential. Bureaucracy flows so easily out of the management concept, yet nothing is so injurious to the human spirit as impersonal and impenetrable bureaucracy. Until some better form of organiza-tion and administration of the church-related college is found— and we should search for one—great effort must be made to re-spect and encourage each of the individuals living and working at the college, and to unite them to each other in a meaningful and rewarding way.

The academic community has long had its own style of governance, namely, the concept of collegiality. While the cor-porate and industrial communities have often criticized the col-legial approach to governance, recently industry has come to take a second look at the concept of collegiality because it treats people with more dignity; people "function" with greater pride and more meaning, and they are more "productive." The church-related college ought to have as one of its cardinal features the concept of collegiality. It is one of the few areas of administration which has withstood the Cartesian-Newtonian paradigm.

The church-related college should spend time and energy maintaining a sense of community on the campus. Life is so frag-mented and impersonal in our society. Under the encouragement of the Christian tenets and the post-modern science paradigm, the church-related college has an opportunity to unite, to tie to-gether, to create fellowship, to provide linkage with other per-sons, and thus to form and maintain a sense of community. Functioning as a community and providing all persons at the col-lege with a sense of belonging, the church-related college can model such community living for a society which seeks anonymity and independence even as it craves a sense of community. Community maintenance ought to be a high priority among all members of the college community. This is an important principle and a most basic human need.

The Christian tenets also suggest an alternative way of living and working together, one that grows out of collegiality and community. American society operates on the basis of "contract theory." Contract theory, at least as we have used it in our litigious society, is based upon an adversarial relationship between persons. Contract theory implies a basic distrust which is overcome only through the creation of a binding legal contract for which, if broken, there are penalties. Contract theory has come to pervade academe, including the church-related college. But contract theory is not consistent with a sense of community, nor with Christian tenets. In place of contract theory, I propose that the church-related college adopt the concept of "covenant." A covenant has a strong biblical basis and requires mutual respect and trust. A covenant treats each person not as an adversary, but as a partner. Covenantal partners are friends who seek each other's well-being. The covenant lies behind the concept of collegiality.

Again, it is very difficult to make the leap from contract theory to a covenantal basis of operation within a society so wedded to contract theory and in such a litigious mood. Nevertheless, I challenge the church-related college to adopt the covenantal model. Let the church-related college contribute this more humane and constructive approach to relationships within our society.

The covenantal approach contains some challenges. Pursuing the covenantal model, church-related colleges will have to attempt to rid themselves of the "we" vs. "they" syndrome which is pervasive in society and also in collegiate life. St. Paul's assertion that we are all one even though we have differing gifts and functions should be taken seriously. The labor-management approach which has encroached upon the college campus should be replaced with a covenantal approach. Here let me call to mind an illustration from the Reformed family of churches. When an infant in a Reformed church is baptized, the entire congregation stands and promises that each will participate in the nurture of the infant until adulthood. A sense of ownership and responsibility is confessed and taken on by the congregation. The care of the infant is the responsibility not only of the parents but also of the congregation. In covenantal relationships on the campus, there ought to be a similar feeling of ownership of and responsibility for each person on the campus.

Let me suggest that church-related colleges adopt this approach to relationships within the campus. Let the colleges find as many ways as possible to replace a contractual approach with a covenantal approach. One area might be tenure. Academic freedom ought to be automatic and assumed at a church-related college. But going beyond academic freedom, church-related colleges should consider operating on the basis of covenants. In place of our current tenure system, we would establish a covenantal system. Great care should be taken initially in the recruitment of personnel—faculty members and administrators. But after a person has been brought into the community, that person's well-being, that person's success, ought to be the focus of attention, indeed the responsibility of the community. The community ought to so nurture, so care for, so include that person that he or she blossoms, and is able to contribute his or her unique personality, work, and other gifts to the community. Instead of putting a person through the lonely, impersonal, anxiety-producing experience of working for tenure, the community ought to adopt a sense of ownership, a sense of responsibility for the care, nurture, and success of that person. This type of caring atmosphere ought to permeate the community.

If a church-related college is to be a Christian community—as, indeed, I believe it should strive to be—then a series of activities similar to the activities of a regular congregation are necessary. A church-related college ought to engage in corporate worship. The college community ought to gather on the campus on a regular basis to engage in corporate worship *as a college community.* Worship is one of the central attributes and activities of the church. For the college to be a Christian community, it should point to the source of life and salvation; it should dramatize what it believes. This is done through corporate worship. Worship of

God in Christ by the entire college is what forms the boundaries of the community; worship gives the college its identity. Worship is what draws the community together, links one member of the college community to the other. Worship, the praise of God in Christ, the preaching and hearing of the Word of God, provides the community with its bonding. From worship flows a caring attitude toward one another, including forgiveness and affirmation. Church-related colleges who wish to take the Christian faith seriously will also take corporate worship seriously.

Christian fellowship flows from a common commitment, in this case a common commitment to God in Christ as well as a common commitment to the learning process. The church-related college can and should be a place where people are cared for even while they are stretched as learners. A church-related college ought to be a place where the individual student, faculty member, and staff member is not lost, forgotten, or excluded; instead, it should be a place where time is taken to become acquainted, where life is personalized through individual attention, and where the well-being of each person is the concern of the entire community.

It ought to be a goal within the church-related college that everyone is entitled to the care and nurture of the college community. The terms "clinical" and "pastoral" might prove helpful in describing my point. Some colleges take a clinical approach to students; just as a doctor waits for patients to come to his or her office, so some faculty members and administrators wait for students to take the initiative and seek out assistance. No responsibility is felt for others unless those persons seek assistance. In contrast to this attitude is the pastoral approach. Once a person joins a congregation, the pastor—and all of the people as extensions of the pastor—can take the initiative in promoting the well-being of that and every other member of the congregation. The pastor can and must take responsibility for his or her congregation, and in order to do so effectively and completely he or she must at times take the initiative in offering care. Falling short of *in loco parentis,* this pastoral model does not seek to dominate or control, but neither does it isolate or neglect. It is a wise, caring approach based upon a covenant relationship to which an individual commits herself when she joins the community. The church-related college can make the academic community into a unique and humane place and, at the same time, provide a model of this approach to human relationships for our society.

Because it is a learning community, the church-related college must give a significant amount of attention to the discussion of moral and ethical topics. Because of its Christian identity and mission, the church-related college ought to be on the cutting edge—for the church and for society—of moral and ethical issues. The college should seek to understand and explain both historic and emerging ethical and moral issues. It should seek to gain a commitment from its students, as part of their Christian faith, to pursue ethical and moral behavior while they are students and when they enter adult society. In all of its institutional activities and dealings, the college should seek to model ethical and moral behavior. It should attempt to help our society grasp the nature of the current moral and ethical dilemmas we face in our society and world, and should, in some way, seek to persuade our society to act in a moral and ethical manner. Because the college is primarily an *educational* institution rather than a social or political institution, its primary focus should be an intellectual one. It should attempt to help the college community understand the ethical and moral issues, rather than striving to be an agent for social and political change. Yet as a Christian institution, it should strive to influence its students toward responsible, ethical, and moral behavior. As an institution affiliated with the church, the college cannot blind its eyes to issues of justice. The college does exist within a society and a world. Therefore at times the church-related college must take a corporate stand within our society and our world on moral and ethical issues in order to maintain its own moral integrity and be true to its Christian identity.

In addition to pursuing moral and ethical issues, a church-related college ought to provide various kinds and levels of programming for the spiritual growth of its members—students, faculty members, and members of the administrative staff. The religious-life programs of church-related colleges unfortunately have been profoundly influenced by the Cartesian-Newtonian paradigm, with the focus on enhancing the spiritual life of the individual student. Consequently, these colleges unwittingly have been promoting the private approach to faith so prevalent in American society. Major Christian tenets and the post-modern science paradigm suggest a different approach, one that focuses on the connectedness among Christians in the church.

Whitworth College is currently designing its religious-life program within a conceptual framework that is informed by Christian tenets and the post-modern science paradigm. The result is a more holistic rather than individualistic and private approach to students. Rather than approaching students as isolated Christians, leaving it up to them to make connections with other Christians, Whitworth's new design connects students with the church by conceiving of the student at the outset as being a part of the church. The student in Christian community is the starting point of this design.

This approach is based upon a strong doctrine of the church and the Protestant concept of the priesthood of all believers. Students are nurtured within the church; they see themselves as connected to and responsible for others, not as isolated individuals. At their core and from the very beginning, students interact with others. Out of this connectedness the students develop a greater sense of wholeness and sense of responsibility for others. In this framework, the curriculum and other forms of programming are designed to approach the students as members of the church; indeed, it prepares them for leadership in the church. The New Testament shows Christ calling disciples into a fellowship as they enact their discipleship. It is as a result of the Cartesian paradigm and America's unique private approach to faith that colleges slipped away from a fundamental doctrine of the church and the Protestant notion of the priesthood of all believers.

A full range of courses flow from this new conceptual framework as part of a program which helps acquaint the participants with the Christian faith—its Hebrew and Jewish background, the biblical literature, the history of Christianity, the relationship between Christianity and the other major religions, Christian liturgy, hymnology, and contemplative literature, along with historical and contemporary theology. In addition, there are discussion groups for the study of books and helpful topics. These are provided for faculty and staff members as well as students. Weekly discussion groups, periodic off-campus retreats, and prayer and meditation sessions aid in the spiritual growth of all members of the college community

As a Christian community, the college community ought to engage in activities which provide a service to others. While they are in college, students ought to learn to take responsibility for others so that when they enter adult society, they will carry this sense of responsibility with them. Faculty and staff members ought to demonstrate how they as adult members of society and as Christians take responsibility for their society, particularly for the less fortunate. Such service projects may begin with assistance for one another on the campus, but they should branch out into the community around the college and into the larger society. Tutoring can be given to fellow students or to students in the local school district. Care for the environment can be given through recycling projects in which the college community participates. The elderly in the surrounding community can overcome their loneliness through the companionship offered by members of the college community. In addition, the elderly often need some assistance with transportation for necessary shopping trips. Students can be of assistance in welfare projects already organized by the local agencies. These are just a few illustrations. It will not take much effort for a college to find areas and agencies within the local community where service is needed. Such service to others is a necessary expression of the Christian faith and therefore a necessary part of the life of a church-related college.

This leads to the topic of a college's ethos. Every college has an ethos. The ethos of a college is the sum total of all of the values, traditions, attitudes, and practices which together function in a unique balance and proportion at that particular college. The ethos of a college is that college's greatest treasure. It is the ethos which shapes the student. It is the ethos which creates the workplace for faculty members, administrators, and students. The ethos works quietly, almost imperceptibly, upon all who live and work at the college. It is the ethos which the alumni of a particular college consciously and unconsciously remember. It is critically important that all members of the college community seek to maintain and enrich the ethos, even as they are its beneficiaries. With the loss of chapel services, which in earlier decades brought all students, faculty members, and administrators together into one place at one time at least several times each week, a large number of church-related colleges lost one of the most effective ways of building and transmitting their ethos. Other ways must be found to nurture and communicate the college's ethos. This is one of the most important agenda items of the future for church-related colleges. Additional effort must be put into finding new ways of maintaining, enriching, communicating, and instilling the college's ethos. No other factor binds the college community together or embodies and transmits the college's unique mission more than a college's ethos.

This chapter contains a significant number of suggestions as to how church-related colleges may build their identities and programs upon Christian tenets and the post-modern science paradigm. Additional suggestions are needed, and I encourage readers to make them. However, just pursuing the ones listed in this chapter presents an imposing challenge. In thinking about this challenge I am reminded of a cartoon by Shel Silverstein. Two convicts are housed in a very high, narrow cell. Near the ceiling far above them is a tiny window, too small for any human to pass through. In addition, they are chained to the wall at three places—arms, neck, and abdomen. In this totally hopeless situation, one of the convicts says to the other, "Now, here's my plan." The challenges to the church-related college are not that enormous, but they are significant. But the reward of pursuing these suggestions will be like acquiring freedom—in this case, freedom to offer a unique college experience to tomorrow's youth.

9. The College's Influence in the Church and in American Society

The thesis of this chapter is that the church-related college has much to offer the mainline Protestant denominations and American society. I will focus first on what the college can offer the church.

The church and the college live on a two-way street. It is a street, however, on which a diminished amount of traffic has traveled during the decades since World War II. It should be clear from all that has been written in the earlier chapters that I believe that both college and church can be greatly enriched if a stronger relationship is formed between these two historic partners.

It goes without saying that the church has much to offer the college; indeed, the college needs the church. The college needs the Christian tenets which are transmitted, in part, by the church. The college needs the church's students. Less than five percent of the students from mainline Protestant denominations attend their church's colleges. If it were not for Catholic, fundamentalist, and nonaligned students, many of the church-related colleges might not be in existence. These colleges need their denomination's students. The church-related colleges also need a higher level of financial support from their denominations. While denominations vary, the funds coming from the denominations to their colleges often amounts to less than one percent of the college's annual budget. This level of financial support for the colleges is not enough to keep the relationship between the two partners strong. The college also needs the interest, concern, and positive criticism of the church. Such interest can only enhance the partnership and serve to enrich the college. But the main purpose of this chapter is not to discuss what the church can and should do for the college. I'll leave that topic for someone else to explore in greater depth or for discussion groups to pursue. My purpose is to describe how the college can and should assist the church.

Before pursuing this topic, however, let me make one additional comment. One very wholesome development has taken place between the two partners since the Second World War, namely, a more mature way in which the colleges and the denominations relate to each other and work together. Several of the mainline Protestant denominations, drawing upon their theological traditions, have developed covenantal relationships between themselves and their colleges. Such covenantal relationships have led to more mature working relationships, replacing the traditional struggle for control and domination which had for many decades marked and marred the relationship between church and college. These new covenantal relationships are a mark of maturity and will prove to be beneficial to college and church. Each is a free, equal partner concerned about, interested in, and seeking the welfare of the other. These covenantal relationships have cleared the air of distrust and have created a new, pleasant, and productive climate between the two partners.

Another result is of equal, if not greater, importance. It is precisely this covenantal relationship, with the freedom which it gives the church-related college, that places the college on solid footing in the higher education arena. The freedom from control and the freedom to pursue the truth, which is at the very core of the covenantal relationship, are the factors which insure the credibility of the church-related college as an *educational institution*. The purpose of the church-related college is education, not indoctrination. Freedom insures an open pursuit of the truth, as opposed to the inculcation of a particular point of view from an external source. Is not the church-related college which has such freedom as credible as, or more credible than, the public university with its often unacknowledged secular point of view? Two factors put the church-related college in an advantageous position: first, the unmasking of the so-called "value-free" point of view, and second, the freedom and credibility which the covenantal relationship gives to the church-related college.

Let us now turn to the ways in which the college can aid the church. Once again, readers are invited to add their own ideas to those offered in this chapter.

Because the college is an educational institution, in some ways isolated from the rush of contemporary life, because traffic in thoughts and ideas is the college's purpose, and because the college is a safe, friendly place where the church can make itself vulnerable, the college can aid the church in its "thinking" process, which Hannah Arendt so eloquently and profoundly describes. This thinking process is absolutely necessary if the church is to be the "leaven" in our society that it is called to be. At the college and in the college, the church has the opportunity to be "absent from the present," to be "absentminded," so that the present can be viewed from a distance. It is so easy for the church to be too deeply influenced by the culture in which it exists and to which it must, in some ways, adapt. It is precisely this gift of helping the church to see its cultural milieu from a distance which will—as Hannah Arendt says—keep the church from becoming banal.[1] The college can help to ensure that there is a contradiction between the church and American culture. In addition, because the college is a place aside, it can be a place of solitude for the church, a change of venue, a place where important ideas are discussed, books are read, and reflection is undertaken. The college can offer the church some extremely valuable time—time away, time to think, time to correct, and time to put oneself back in touch with one's center, primary sources, and purpose.

Since the college and the church are equal partners who seek each other's welfare within a covenantal relationship, each can serve as "conscience" to the other. Since we are focusing on

1. Hannah Arendt, *Thinking* (New York: Harcourt Brace Jovanovich, 1978), p. 4.

how the college can assist the church, the college can serve as a conscience to the church. It is not that the college's role is to tell the church that it is wrong on a particular issue. Rather, the college is a place where discussion of many important issues takes place, particularly value issues that are on the leading edge of society. That is the work of the college. Such discussion is a natural part of being a liberal-arts, church-related college. Questions pertaining to justice, the arms race, human rights, human dignity, hunger, business ethics, medical ethics, and biological engineering—to begin the list—are discussed on campus as an integral part of the learning program. Students thereby become more conscious of such issues; they are taught how to approach such issues and shown Christian approaches to addressing such issues. As colleges address these issues with their students, they are indirectly sharing such views with the church and thereby serving as its conscience. By the same token, as these issues are addressed in the church, the church may serve as conscience to the colleges. As partners, each should attempt to help the other be as sensitive, sharp, and analytic as possible in pursuing the implications of the Christian faith. Just as individual members of a family may be helped through a discussion of a particular issue around the dinner table, so discussions at the colleges and within the church will aid these two family members. Furthermore, issues pursued in community and dialogue will be better addressed than issues pursued in isolation. The church and the college ought to work together, in tandem, in order to produce creative dialogue, so that they address issues as fully and as faithfully as possible.

One of the most significant, long-term ways in which the college should aid the church is in pursuing the theological implications of the post-modern science paradigm. In a manner of speaking, a paradigm puts a certain set of glasses on a culture so that everything which that culture sees is through that set of glasses. Those glasses also allow a culture to see certain things and not see other things. The glasses not only screen in or out, but also encourage a certain perspective and discourage another perspective. A culture's theological activity is as influenced by such glasses as are all of the other dimensions of that culture.

The Christian faith has lived under several paradigms; it has pursued its theological work wearing several different sets of glasses in different periods of history. These different sets of glasses in different eras have determined the theological results. The Christian message as understood and transmitted by the apostles and the earliest Christians was a product of the glasses bestowed by Hebrew culture. The Hebrews focused on God's activity among humankind in everyday life, perceiving God and transmitting their understanding of him in story form. Their perception of God was a very anthropomorphic image. Their stories focused upon God's activity on behalf of the Hebrew people. They saw the love of God intersecting with key figures in Hebrew history. The gospels of the New Testament are very much the products of the oral culture which typified Hebrew life.

When Christianity moved to the Greco-Roman world, it traveled beyond the boundaries of the Hebrew paradigm. At first Christianity had to adapt the way its message was conceived and presented to the way in which the Greco-Roman mind perceived reality and the way it worked. Later, as Christianity took root in the Greco-Roman world, the transfer from the Hebrew paradigm to the Greco-Roman paradigm became complete, permanent, *and normative.* When Constantine converted to Christianity and made it the state religion, still another dimension was added to the way in which Christian theology was done; an imperial dimension was added, in keeping with the Greco-Roman paradigm.

The effect of a paradigm on the Christian faith is not to make it more or less correct under one paradigm or another, only different. In fact, a change in a paradigm, while caused by the changed mind-set or consciousness of the people—or, as in the case of the change in paradigm from Hebrew culture to Greco-Roman culture, by a move of the major locus of the faith—may be beneficial to the faith. To linger too long under one particular paradigm may be harmful, not unlike pushing a metaphor too far. A paradigm lasts until it is no longer useful. This is the case with the Cartesian-Newtonian paradigm. It has become more harmful than helpful, not just to scientists, but to theologians as well.

We are living at a time when we are changing our paradigm. Our view of reality is changing. New theories of reality will simply no longer fit into the Cartesian-Newtonian paradigm. This has forced scientists to perceive reality in a new and different way. As a result, the view of reality held by the average person is in the process of changing and will be changing for a considerable period of time. In years to come we will be different people; that is, we will perceive reality differently than we have in the past, and as a result, our consciousness will be different. New ideas and perceptions will open up to us because we will be donning a new pair of glasses. The Christian faith must adapt to this new paradigm, for it will have to do new theological work under this new paradigm. Indeed, new vistas will open up to Christian theology.

The view of reality in the post-modern science paradigm is very different from the view of reality in the Cartesian-Newtonian paradigm. There will be some exciting, helpful changes, but there will also be some significant challenges. Certain aspects of the Christian faith which have only played a minor part may come into prominence, and some aspects which have played a major role under the old paradigm may recede in importance. For example, under the old paradigm God's unchanging nature played a significant role in our understanding of God. In the future, with a view of the universe as in a state of becoming, a perception of God as unchanging may diminish, or even be a roadblock. Under the Cartesian-Newtonian paradigm, God was removed from a machinelike universe, which was created and set in motion to follow endlessly the laws of nature. In the new paradigm, the universe is perceived to be in a state of becoming, and therefore more attention will have to be paid to the concept of creativity—God's creative activity and man's creative activity. And with such an open-ended concept of reality, the Holy Spirit may become a much more meaningful dimension of the Trinity than before.

How will theologians handle this different perception, these different emphases? How will the church be affected, either negatively or positively, by this new paradigm? The church did not fare very well under the Cartesian-Newtonian paradigm, largely because the church did not handle the rise of science very well. The Cartesian-Newtonian paradigm was hard on Christianity, and in some ways victimized it. But we also have to say that the church did not handle the challenge of the Cartesian-Newtonian paradigm very well. Therefore, it is essential that the church meet the challenge of this change in paradigm. The Christian faith may fare well under the new paradigm. There are many hopeful signs: the spiritual dimension of mankind is at least acknowledged, the new paradigm sees mystery in the physical realm, and the physical universe is seen as unified—all of which are consonant with major Christian tenets. And the very fact that the church will have an almost overwhelming amount of theological "homework" to do in adapting to this new paradigm means that the church must once again focus heavily upon theology. This can only benefit the church.

What a great challenge the church-related college faces in assisting the church to move into the new paradigm! I encourage the church-related college to adopt this project over the next few decades, to assist the church in understanding the new paradigm—a challenge in itself—and to help the church shape a Christian faith whose ambience will be the consciousness growing out of this new paradigm. Let the church-related college and the church as partners get on with this exciting and extremely important task.

The church-related college can and should enrich the church's culture. During the decades since the Second World War, with the widening gap between the church-related college and the church, the influence which the college historically had upon the church has waned. As we noticed, most of the clergy in the mainline Protestant denominations attended a public university, in sharp contrast to the practice of previous decades when clergy were the product of the church-related colleges. The same pattern came to be true of the laity. If the church will send more of its young people to the church-related colleges, these young people will carry the ethos of the colleges with them. They will be familiar with, even practiced in, the church's culture, which is a vital part of the life of the church-related college. The church-related college produces clergy and laity alike who are biblically literate and acquainted with and committed to handling the ethical and moral issues facing the church and society. Church-related college graduates will be products of a caring community who therefore will bring a sense of wholeness and community to the church. They will also have well-integrated and purposeful lives and be practiced leaders who wish to be of service to the church and society.

There is, however, an even greater challenge which, if accepted by the college, will significantly enrich the mission and culture of the church. I challenge the church-related college intentionally to adopt an attitude and a program to practice and experiment with, thereby enhancing the church's culture on campus. Such activity will enrich its own life and also enrich the culture of the church. I challenge the colleges to use, experiment with, and create music, drama, art, and literature as means of enhancing the life of the church. In addition, I challenge the colleges to pursue theological, ethical, and moral topics to enrich the lives of their students and the life of the church. Finally, I encourage the churches to call upon faculty members to assist in the programs of the church, and to assist the churches with their overall mission and direction. These faculty members are a too little used resource who wish to give a gift of their particular talents to the church. As covenantal partners, the college and the church can and should enrich the other. Each will benefit.

The church-related college which pursues its unique identity and mission seriously and with vigor will offer American society a much-needed alternative form of education. American society will be greatly enriched by church-related colleges if these colleges carry out their individual missions with purposefulness and integrity. Let me close this chapter and the book with a description of how the church-related college can enrich American society in the future.

Instead of being "value free," the church-related college is "value laden." Instead of somewhat unconsciously accepting a secular point of view, the student at the church-related college receives a great deal of practice in wrestling with values. As a result, the graduate of the church-related college is more conscious of her value system, and has spent more time putting in place an enriched and integrated value system than a graduate of a secular university. Time is spent in the curriculum and through intentional student-life programming at the church-related college in helping the student develop a philosophy of life. Thus, when the student enters society after college, she will have direction and purpose in her life. Spending time in developing the whole student, the church-related college assists her in developing a personal vision of what she can become and her place in society, as well as a vision for a better society. Accompanying that vision are ideals for the student as well as for society. Instead of saying that this very personal dimension of the student is off-limits, the church-related college takes responsibility for developing and enriching this dimension of the student. A secular education—one which fails to focus on this spiritual dimension—leaves this dimension of the student stunted. The cumulative effect upon society is a spiritual vacuum, an aimless and value-confused society. But the church-related college sends into society a purposeful, enriched, full person who in turn shapes, directs, and enriches our society.

Instead of promoting a secular view of life, the church-related college encourages the development and enrichment of the Christian faith in its students. Transcendence is the major tenet upon which the church-related college is based, in contrast to the non-transcendent point of view of the secular university. Enriching the Christian faith of the students leads to a certain kind of student, a certain quality of graduate who brings certain kinds of characteristics to society.

A student who is well-grounded in the Christian faith has a basis, a foundation from which springs his ethics. Currently some universities, private and public, are seeking to add a course in ethics to the curriculum at these universities. While such courses may help a student understand ethics, they do not necessarily cause students to adopt an ethical stance for themselves.

A person's ethics must flow from a belief system of personal commitment and conviction. It is unfortunate that we believe we can simply tack on a course in ethics and expect persons thereafter to behave ethically. One value to society of the church-related college is that graduates come to society with a belief system which is the source of their ethics. Society is enhanced by such graduates.

A college education which includes the goal of enriching the spiritual dimension of its students will produce graduates who have spiritual resources for their lives as well as for the society in which they live. American society, which is so materialistic and so focused on the pursuit of instant gratification and on quick results, will be enhanced by graduates who are more spiritual, reflective, and thoughtful, whose spirituality helps them to critique American society, and who bring this spirituality with them into society.

Church-related colleges inform their students of their responsibility toward their fellowman and offer them opportunities to serve others. The Christian faith calls its adherents to service. Such graduates will temper America's current individualism and reawaken America's historic concern for those who need assistance.

The church-related college also produces graduates who, because of their faith, have an understanding of and concern for our shrinking world. The Christian faith overlooks political boundaries as well as the traditional boundaries of race and sex. Our shrinking, delicate world needs persons who have this larger, more integrated vision of humanity. The church-related college also produces graduates who, because of their faith, are stewards of the world's delicate ecological system, of its limited resources, of its many peoples, and of the world's beauty. The issues of peace, food, shelter, justice, and human freedom—issues flowing from the Christian faith—are on the minds of the graduates of the church-related college.

Because they focus on the spiritual dimension of students, the church-related colleges provide American society with people who have depth, who have in their faith a touchstone for their

lives, who have a point of view, who have motivation and purpose in their lives, and who have a mandate from their faith to
take responsibility for their society and their world.

Most church-related colleges are relatively small colleges.
This allows them, by choice, to offer a more personalized approach to education. Students can receive the attention they need
and desire. Instead of being treated as part of a mass, each student can be treated with the dignity of individual attention. The
result is that students feel their personal worth. They become acquainted with their teachers, which serves to enhance the educational enterprise. They can tailor the curriculum to their individual needs under the guidance of a faculty advisor. Instead
of being just a number and being caught in a bureaucracy, students at church-related colleges can blossom. Where they are
known and appreciated as individual human beings, students can
develop their unique individual talents and skills. Such a personalized approach to education not only assists students, but
also helps to make our society more humane. The church-related
college is a part of the solution to our often dehumanizing society.

Students who attend these small colleges have the advantage that, in addition to a personalized experience with the curriculum, they can also participate in a variety of extracurricular
activities. Here social skills are sharpened, particularly leadership
skills. Throughout their four years, students can rise from simple
participation to leadership, serving as organizers, officers, direc-
tors, etc. The result is a graduate who has a high level of self-
esteem and self-confidence and who has the ability therefore to
translate leadership from the college scene into her profession
and into her community. Our society benefits from an educational
process which develops leadership that so quickly translates into
society.

Those church-related colleges which take the Christian
faith seriously and work from the paradigm of integration develop a "sense of community" on their campuses. Students who
attend these colleges have been the beneficiaries of care and concern and they know the benefits of this more personalized approach to life. When they enter society after graduation, they take

with them this approach to life. It counters the prevalent separation, isolation, loneliness, and individualism. Thus they bring to our society a necessary correction, an ingredient which helps to personalize our society and to bring it a greater sense of community. Society is richer because of the integration, connectedness, and care which the graduates of the church-related colleges bring with them.

Because the church-related colleges are committed not only to strengthening and enriching the "moral virtues" of their students but also to excellence in the "intellectual virtues," they provide the type of excellence in education which recent national studies have been seeking in order to strengthen American higher education. A glance at some recent national rankings of liberal arts colleges shows that a host of church-related colleges are among those liberal arts colleges which receive the highest ranking for academic excellence. The church-related college has a record of excellence in the past and is committed to even greater academic excellence in the future. These colleges have served our society well in the past and will continue to keep American higher education the best system of higher education in the world.

Just as the church-related college has an excellent academic reputation, it also has an excellent record of educating minority students. Earlier in this book I indicated that in the state of Ohio, the private colleges have a higher percentage of minority students than do the public universities. Unfortunately this is a well-kept secret, and obviously more must be done in the future. But it can be said somewhat proudly that the church-related colleges assist society through the education of minority students.

The church-related colleges have a particular role to play in our pluralistic society. America cannot allow pluralism to mean that society is based upon the lowest common denominator of agreement. Pluralism cannot mean that differences are played down for our society to function. Rather, a pluralistic society will work and will be rich and vibrant if the various groups and points of view will share their richness and unique point of view in a spirit of understanding and tolerance. It is from this vantage point that the church-related college can play a significant role in enriching America as a pluralistic society. The church-related college acquaints its students with the Judeo-Christian tradition and seeks to enrich their understanding of and commitment to the Christian tenets. When these students enter adult society, they bring with them a distinct, enriched point of view rather than no point of view or a bland secular point of view. Our society is enriched by persons who are acquainted with their heritage and who live on the basis of a conscious, well-informed faith and value system. Particularly those church-related colleges which give attention to the changing issues of "Christ and culture" will provide society with informed graduates who will commit themselves to enriching American society.

The church-related college also assists American society by participating in the conscience of society. So many profound ethical issues face society. The issues of truth, integrity, peace, justice, poverty, hunger, and race are now joined by ethical issues created by advanced technology—in the fields of medicine and bioengineering, for example. The church-related colleges are discussing these issues on campus. They are training students in all of the professions to think about their own personal ethics, ethical issues in their professions, and the broad ethical issues in society. The ethical point of view with which the graduates of church-related colleges enter society has the Christian faith as its foundation, rather than having a secular foundation or being based on personal feelings. Therefore the church-related college is a rich resource for ethical leadership in our society.

The church-related colleges have played an historic role in the church and in American society in the past. Both the church and contemporary American society will benefit in the future from those church-related colleges which pursue their unique identity and mission with purposefulness and integrity.